ALFRED NISBETT left school at fourteen and, apart from the war years, spent most of his working life in the furniture trade. It wasn't until his retirement and after much encouragement from his wife and daughters that he finally wrote his story, recalling the kindness of strangers who became lifelong friends.

Always Tomorrow
Sempre Domani

Always Tomorrow
Sempre Domani

Alfred Nisbett

ATHENA PRESS
LONDON

ALWAYS TOMORROW
Sempre Domani
Copyright © Alfred Nisbett 2008

All Rights Reserved

No part of this book may be reproduced in any form
by photocopying or by any electronic or mechanical means,
including information storage or retrieval systems,
without permission in writing from both the copyright
owner and the publisher of this book.

ISBN 978 1 84748 319 5

First published 2008 by
ATHENA PRESS
Queen's House, 2 Holly Road
Twickenham TW1 4EG
United Kingdom

Printed for Athena Press

The author would like to express his great appreciation for all the help and really hard work that Ann Killingback has put into my being able to finish this book.

Chapter One

Having arrived home from the post office after collecting my old-age pension, I was sitting, thinking of times past and, frankly, wondering where the years had gone. At the age of sixty-seven, to remember yourself as a teenager is a very sobering thought. However, it is amazing how clearly one can recollect so much of what happened so many years ago.

Childhood is, of course, the usual starting point. People have very different opinions on the subject of schooldays. Members of my family have let me know, in no uncertain terms, how much they hated that part of their lives. I have formed the opinion, from talking to my own children, that the main factor causing this attitude was the quality of their teachers.

We had the greatest respect for our teachers, because they certainly invoked rigid discipline. In those days, if a pupil stepped out of line, he or she was punished. The punishment meted out was, from my observations, generally well deserved. These were not, in my opinion, in any way brutal or sadistic. I recall that, in the Infants, it was usually a slapped wrist. For more serious infractions came a slap around the legs and then the final punishment was to be sent to the Headmaster's study to collect the punishment book and the cane. If anything of this nature occurred today there would be an outcry. It is, I think, a sign of the times when we see all around us the vandalism, hooliganism, graffiti and litter abounding in our country, no matter where you go. This, to me, clearly shows the lack of respect some younger people have for their elders and others have for their property and the environment.

I know that if my father were alive today he would be apoplectic. He was a true working-class person, as, indeed, was my mother. When I was a child, his job was working on road maintenance. What a soul-destroying job that was, to be sure! When he was working near our home I would go along to watch him and his gang. There would be one man holding a long tool resembling a pair of pincers, and in the pincers would be a metal chisel, about one foot in length. He would hold the chisel over the required spot on the road and the other three members of the gang would take up their sledgehammers and start swinging. Thump! Thump! Thump! It was really hard physical labour for the magnificent reward of two pounds a week. He did this for many years and one day I remember him telling my mother that at long last he could get out of the rain because he had got a new job. The council had built some new toilets and he had applied for the position of attendant and been successful. He was really pleased that there would be no more of that awful slogging on the roads!

Money was always a very real problem in our family. This was nothing unusual in those days; it was almost as though it was accepted as a fact of life. Very many people had little money and found life extremely hard. This was when we British were the richest and most powerful country in the world. Yet the poverty that existed was widespread. I recall my father saying to me, 'Son, the better-off just do not care one iota for the position of the poorer among the population. But there is just one exception to that rule, and that is when they declare war on whoever – then a great change comes about. Overnight this poor, overlooked section of the community becomes "our lads".'

How very true. I have experienced this myself during my lifetime. My father did 'his bit' in World War I. He was wounded and, after a period of convalescence, was sent to Northern Ireland. He told me that he hated every moment he was there, which on reflection is hardly surprising, considering that when he was in France he was just seventeen years old. When he was finally demobilised he said he ceased to be one of 'our lads' and became one of the unemployed. Before obtaining his job with the local council, his attitude, he told me, was very bitter indeed. The reason was that they all thought they would return to a 'land fit for heroes' and of course this just did not happen. It was simply back to square one.

By the time I was due to leave school at the age of fourteen, my father had been in his new council job some two years. He knew that he was a very fortunate man to have a job to get up to in the morning.

I found employment with a furniture manufacturer as a trainee cabinet maker; my rate of pay was two and a half pence per hour. That is, of course, in the old currency. It was a forty-eight-hour week so my total pay was ten shillings per week. From this I had a deduction of four pence for a National Insurance stamp so I proudly carried home nine shillings and eight pence to my mother, who gave me back two shillings for myself. Pocket money – I was rich!

The next few years passed by and history was about to repeat itself, with gathering war clouds. Herr Hitler was shouting his stupid head off and I guess we all knew it was going to happen again. In 1938 we had Mr Chamberlain visiting Hitler and returning with his now-famous piece of paper. Even with this piece of paper, the preparations for war went on apace. At my factory we were busily engaged in producing ammunition boxes.

Anyone with the least scrap of grey matter could see that it was just a matter of time before we would be embroiled in another European war. By now I was nineteen years old and I had met my future wife and was pursuing her very resolutely. But nothing was going to be allowed to proceed normally. The war was getting closer and closer.

About this time, if I remember correctly, the government under Mr Neville Chamberlain introduced a scheme for military service, which became known as 'the Militia'. Young men were going to be called up to do so many months' service with the armed forces. It was possible to avoid this call-up by joining the Territorial Army. Now, there were many young men who had no desire whatever to be called up, so they flocked to join the Territorials. Many of my age group were among them and of course when war broke out they were the first to receive their calling-up papers. So, on 3 September 1939, the cabinet shop in which I was working was short of quite a few people.

Things were beginning to change quite significantly. Sandbags were being stacked against the walls of the more important buildings in the locality. Every lorry that passed by was daubed with the initials 'W.D.' The sky was hung with barrage balloons.

People were being issued with gas masks and ration cards. There was a great sense of urgency in the air, and also a feeling of wondering what was going to happen next.

For quite some time, nothing of any great importance did happen, not in France anyway. It was the time that became known as the 'phoney war'. One event that did take place on 3 September 1939 was the German sinking of a passenger ship, the *Athenia*, with a great loss of life. This action by the Germans caused an immense feeling of horror throughout the country. The ship was carrying mainly women and children across the Atlantic. I suppose one could say that this occurrence really brought it home to us that we were at war with a country that would do absolutely anything to gain its own ends.

People were discovering that life would now be changing for them. They were finding that they had a ritual every evening, fixing the blackout around the home. When they went out, they had to remember to pick up their cardboard box containing their gas mask. With the sirens beginning to wail out their warnings and everybody running for cover, it made you realise, deep down, that we were in for a very trying time indeed.

Meanwhile, I was continuing with my job turning out ammunition boxes to the satisfaction of the government inspector, who was roaming around the factory all day, every day. I was, I suppose, just waiting for my age group to be called up. I was marking time, just waiting for the inevitable to happen.

When the Germans attacked in Belgium, Holland and France, their overwhelming superiority in men and materials saw them through to the coast of France in no time at all. So from 29 May to 4 June 1940, we saw the evacuation of our troops from Dunkirk. Nine days later I was to report to Shorncliffe Barracks, near Folkestone and Dover, to commence my training as a sapper in the Royal Engineers.

Chapter Two

So it was that on 13 June 1940 I found myself in an Army barracks and going through the procedures, as was to be the lot of so many thousands of young men. The first thing that struck me was the amount of shouting that was done by the NCOs. I was often to wonder why it was not possible to give an order without bawling it out. The first day was mainly taken up with medical exams and documentation and I got my first look at an Army pay book. I was also given my Army number: 2110225, plus my rank, which was Sapper RE. I had my leg pulled by my mates, when I received my calling-up papers, because I was told to report on the thirteenth, generally looked upon as a very unlucky number. I then noted that if you were to tot up the figures in my Army number they too totalled thirteen. Being superstitious, I should have resigned on the spot, but I was very much aware that the Army would take a dim view of that!

The following day was a Friday and we spent this being kitted out with uniform and equipment, with many a laugh at the 'fit' of most of our uniforms. We were informed that we would be going to see the regimental tailor, who would cut things to shape and also put a decidedly necessary tuck in here and there. When your name came up to see the tailor, you said you had an appointment with 'some here and there'. Being Friday, it was pay day. We were instructed in the ritual of being paid – it was very simple. All you were required to do was step up smartly to the table and salute the officer, then sign the acquittance roll against your name, collect your pay and step back to the ranks. I was getting, so I understood, one shilling a day. I'd been in the Army two days and the acquittance roll said two shillings. So far everything was working out correctly. I then moved one pace sideways to pick up my two bob only to be given one shilling. I queried this. Then there was a great roaring sound in my ear. It was an NCO informing me that I was issued yesterday with eating irons and a dixie to the value of one shilling and that I had to pay for these items. I can to this day remember the fury that raged inside me. To think that they hauled you into the Army to fight a war that you never asked for and you were actually made to pay for a piece of equipment that is absolutely essential to help you eat. The mind boggles!

We were informed that the intake of 150, of which I was part, was to be known as No. 24 War Party. We were then split up into five sections of thirty men and the sections numbered from one to five. To each section we had one full corporal and a lance corporal, whose duty it was to turn us into trained sappers. They told us that they had twelve weeks in which to achieve this. The first thing we had to do was to march to the armoury to collect our weapons. This really was an eye-opener. The weapon I was issued with was a rifle known as a P14, known also, I believe, as a Canadian Ross rifle. It was very, very ancient, but the bayonet still fitted on the end satisfactorily. We could not be issued with a regulation gas mask because they didn't have any, so we retained our civvy masks, each in a cardboard box, dangling down our backs on a piece of string.

Our training now began in earnest. Square-bashing was the first thing to which we were introduced and, surprisingly, I found that I rather liked it. This was something of a shock to me, as I had thought that I would hate it. This was followed by 'weaponry, bridging, demolitions, mine-laying, booby-traps and fieldcraft'. All this was crammed into a twelve-week training course, so it left little time for recreation. In fact, when the day's work was finished, it was an unwritten law that you went to the company notice board to see what was on the orders for the following day.

One thing used to make me hopping mad. This concerned our webbing equipment. One day it would say that we would parade, with equipment 'blancoed' (i.e. whitened), the next day 'scrubbed', the next day 'blancoed' again and so on. So our evenings were taken up in the ablutions, either scrubbing or blancoing our equipment. To us young trainee sappers it was just plain stupidity on the part of those in authority, because all we were doing was wearing out our very good webbing at a fast rate. However, we were sufficiently intelligent to appreciate that, while all this time our evenings were taken up with this activity with our webbing, we hardly had any time to be getting into any sort of mischief anywhere else. There was method in their madness.

After a few weeks had gone by, some parts of our training were reaching their end. The first of these was our square-bashing. We were told that, when we had our passing-out parade, one man from each section would be selected as the star man and he would receive a star to be worn on his denims. I can honestly say that I was deeply embarrassed to receive the star for our section, amid much mickey-taking from my mates.

By now, London was being bombed, and as most of our party were Londoners, we were becoming very agitated indeed. Our training was disrupted because whenever the air-raid siren sounded we had defensive posts to take up; for this we were issued with five rounds of 3.03 ammunition each. I remember thinking what a great help that would be if we were to be invaded!

With our training now completed, we were sent out on detachment to Dover. Here, for our first job as fully fledged sappers, we were to get a nasty surprise. Dover was being bombarded from the French coast. This in itself wasn't at all pleasant. The job we had been given to do was even more unpleasant. Dover has four piers and on the end of each pier was a railway goods wagon, packed with explosives. Our job was a daily check on the condition of the explosives, the wiring and the detonators. Having carried out the checks on the wagon, we then went back to the entrance to the pier, where the exploder box was situated, and waited for the order to hit the box – an order we knew we would get if an invasion were imminent.

We were carrying out our routine checks one morning. It was a lovely sunny day; the barrage balloons were moving slowly to and fro and my mate Bill Armon and I were underneath the truck at the end of the pier. We were replacing a detonator on one of the charges when all hell let loose. The Germans were dive-bombing the harbour and there we were, underneath quite a large amount of extremely dangerous material. I do not exaggerate when I say that I was petrified. The noise was unbelievable and, fortunately for us, the Germans were concentrating on the shipping in the harbour. A number of ships were sunk, mainly small ships. I saw three Jerry aircraft finish up in the Channel. All in all, this was a very frightening experience!

Shortly after this, we were recalled to barracks at Shorncliffe and sent on our very first leave: seven days' embarkation leave. So my first leave was to be my last before departing from England. Of course, we had no idea where we would be going; all that was very hush-hush. At the end of my leave we returned to our barracks at Shorncliffe and, as we had been given embarkation leave, we were all confined to barracks. It would seem that this is accepted procedure in the Army. We spent a very boring couple of weeks there and then one day we were told to get our gear together, as we were on our way. We were on our way only as far as Chatham, and into barracks once more. Again we were told that we were still confined to barracks. Altogether we spent seven weeks in that place, Kitchener Barracks. As we were not a unit of Royal Engineers, just a bunch of sappers who were being sent abroad as reinforcements, we had no colonel, major, captain or lieutenants or NCOs, but we were allotted two second lieutenants and an RSM. These three did actually come abroad with us.

As I've said before, we were predominantly Londoners and, as the Jerries were stepping up their bombing of London, there were quite a lot of the lads going absent. To me this was very understandable; to the powers-that-be this was a heinous crime. So, of course, when the time came to move out we were short of a few sappers. I've often wondered what happened to them.

We were put on a train at around midnight, still with absolutely no idea where we would end up. In the morning, after travelling through the night, the train came to a halt and we were ordered to detrain. We were in Liverpool docks. A very large ship was at the dockside and we all went aboard. Once on board, we discovered the name of the ship, the *Britannic*. This ship had not been converted to being a troopship, so we were quite pleased to find that we were allocated a cabin with four berths. I don't think that there was a man among us who could have guessed that this ship was going to be our billet for the next two and a half months. From information gleaned later, I discovered that the ship left the port of Liverpool and sailed straight across the Atlantic to just off the coast of America. It then proceeded southward down the coast of South America, and then turned east and cut across the South

Atlantic to South Africa, just turned around the Cape, and docked at Durban. The powers-that-be told us that we would be in dock for four days while the ship was refuelled and restocked with supplies, and that we would be getting shore leave by day and reporting back on board each night. There was great jubilation among the lads at being given this news. All along the harbour wall there was a long line of cars. As we left the ship, the owners of these vehicles, the citizens of Durban, were picking us up and whisking us off to their homes. I went with a Mr Brown, who lived at No. 36 Innes Road. He was a gentleman of Scottish descent and he lived in a spacious bungalow with his wife. We had tea with them and then they took us by car to see the valley of a thousand hills, a magnificent sight. With the Brown family being so very hospitable, taking us around, showing us the sights, the four days went by like lightning.

Back on board and preparing to leave Durban, the officers were very busy with roll calls, to find out how many had decided to extend their stay in Durban with a bit of French leave. Quite a few had decided to take this step, but I know that they paid very dearly for it at a later date.

By now the ship's geography was no longer a mystery to us. During the first few days on board, all of us were constantly getting lost in the many passageways and stairs. I think the route we all mastered first was the way to the galley. The food on board was of a reasonable standard, considering the fact that they were carrying about four times the normal number of passengers. The officers, naturally, were on the top decks. We were all down below and it was therefore much warmer in our quarters. When passing through the tropics, it was almost unbearable down below. It became standard practice to vacate the bunk in the evening, find a spot on deck and settle down for the night in the open air. This lasted for just three nights. We were then told that sleeping on deck was prohibited and that we must return to our bunks to sleep.

Now that our journey had resumed, we fell back into the shipboard routine. Every day was a repetition of the previous day – PT, boat drill and duty on the machine guns that had been positioned in all sorts of places around the ship. During off-duty hours, we had the inevitable housey housey. Every so often we would get the alarm: 'Action stations!' Each of us on gun duty would remain at our post while the rest all had to get below deck. I can remember thinking that, if we were to be attacked and hit, those below deck wouldn't be in a very favourable position at all. I can say with all honesty that when we got these alarms my heart rate increased significantly.

There was a considerable feeling of trepidation among the thousands of people on the ship; it might be strange to say that I felt an odd feeling of being cut off. We had now been at sea for about eight weeks with no communication of any sort from home. Of course, we knew that the bombing of London was continuing and thoughts for the safety of my family and my girlfriend were never very far away.

Eventually the ship arrived at our port of disembarkation – Port Suez. To look over the side at all the Arab labourers working in the docks made us realise that we had indeed arrived at a totally different scene from that to which we were accustomed. Once we had left the ship with all our equipment, we had a short march to the railway, where we then boarded the train. This in itself was an eye-opener. The seats and backrest were of wood, as was the carriage. Along the entire length of the train was a milling mass of very smelly Arabs, trying to sell just about everything under the sun. Then the train's whistle sounded, it went forward a few yards, then stopped; then began a terrific scramble by all the Arab spivs to get off the train. It was real pantomime!

Once the train was under way, you could begin to realise what a dreary, desolate place Egypt really was – mile after mile of nothing but scrub and sand, with the occasional native plodding along by the side of the tracks. We arrived at our destination at about 4 p.m., tired, hot, dusty and dirty, at the town called Ismailia. It stank!

Wagons were waiting to transport us to our camp and we piled aboard, only too happy to get away from the pong. The journey was a short one, only about ten miles or so from Ismailia, but at least the smell didn't extend this far. The camp itself consisted of hundreds of tents pitched in sand, and the scenery was just sand – as far as the eye could see in every direction, sand and more sand.

Eventually we were allocated our tents and were able to divest ourselves of all our equipment and begin to look around. The first priority for most of us was to find the latrines. These were situated about one hundred yards from the nearest tent. We discovered that 'latrine' in the local lingo was known as the 'house of good manners'.

This was a very well organised camp in every respect. After our settling into the tent and visiting the latrine, we were able to take a badly needed shower and then it was over to the cookhouse for a meal. This turned out to be something that was going to become very familiar to us. It was stew made from tins of McConachie's meat and veg.

Chapter Three

The following morning we were lectured by the medical officer on the subject of personal hygiene in the Middle East. This was followed by a talk given by a different officer on what was available for us in the way of entertainment. It didn't amount to a great deal. It appears that there was a Mr Shaftoe who owned a chain of cinemas, consisting of tin sheds open to the sky. He showed ancient films that kept wandering off the screen to the accompaniment of ribald comments from the audience. There was also a club called the Copper Kettle, where you could get the usual tea and 'wads', or egg and chips. This place was in Ismailia. Lorries were laid on so that a squaddie could get there about once a week, strictly in rotation.

I had only been in this camp four days when I saw my name come up on Company Orders. I was posted to the 4th Field Squadron REs. I wondered where they were. I was soon to find out. The following morning I, with five of my mates, had to move off to the station in Ismailia for onward travel to Alexandria, where, upon arrival, we were to report to the Station Transport Officer. Upon our reporting to him, we were told that our destination was Mersah Matruh and that the next train for there was not due for two and a half hours. We could, he said, leave our packs and kitbags outside his office and have a look around Alexandria. We didn't need any persuading. Having to hump a small pack, sidearm and rifle each was a bit of a bind so we decided to find the nearest NAAFI to seek some refreshment. We returned to the station in good time. Our kit was outside the office, except we could not actually see it. It was covered in a seething mass of flies. I knew that the MO had mentioned flies with some emphasis, but I had never realised what a problem they were in this country.

Sometime in the late afternoon we reached our destination at Mersah Matruh and were met by a wagon that took us out to our new unit, at a place called Bagush. Here we could see that this unit was in the throes of a quick move and the following morning we were off up the line. The seasoned lads in our new outfit called this 'going up the blue'. I don't know the mileage we did each day; all I do remember is the absolute discomfort of sitting in the back of a fifteen-hundredweight Morris Commercial, caked with a thick layer of dust that you could not do anything about. At night we 'harboured', that is to say that the cookhouse wagon took up a central position and all the company vehicles were surrounding it in a circle, at fifty-yard intervals. This was a precaution against air attack and, as it turned out, a very prudent one indeed. Our first attack occurred on our second night on the road. We had just come to a halt and got into our usual harbouring positions when a bomb went off about half a mile away, followed by others going off even farther away. I couldn't believe it. There was absolutely nothing else within miles of us. On looking up, we could see four aircraft at a tremendous height. They were Italian; we had been baptised, after a style – Italian style. We were soon to discover that the German style was a much more professional approach.

On the third day we were still bowling along the coastal road and had left Sollum, Derna and Tobruk well behind us. As we were approaching Barce, sitting in the back of the truck with my back to the cab, I suddenly realised that aircraft were heading for us out of the sun. I banged on the cab and went over the side and lay very, very still. German fire started to tear into the vehicles about three trucks in front of us. One of them went up in flames immediately. There were four aircraft in this attack. After their first pass, they circled and came in again. This time they went along machine gunning by the sides of the trucks. They knew that was where we were – clever lads!

After the attack, we found that we had lost the truck that caught fire, one sapper had been shot in the leg and two further trucks were no longer of any use to us because they were too badly shot up. After about an hour's delay, we moved off once again, passed through Barce and harboured for the night about fifteen miles into the desert. Throughout this journey, we had passed the debris of the previous battles that had taken place and now we had left a little of our own debris behind us.

The following morning we were headed for Beda Fomm. It was here that a huge tank battle had taken place between our Tank Corps and the Italians. We harboured there among all these knocked-out tanks, the great majority of which were Italian. The following morning we were detailed to clear up the battlefield in company with the Ordnance Corps, who were after salvaging as much as they could from the wrecks that were lying around in abundance. Our task was gruesome. Some of the enemy tanks still had the dead inside them and it was a very unpleasant task to get them out and bury them. In some cases we didn't bother because the people inside were so mutilated that burial was an impossibility, so we cremated them inside the tank. On reflection it must have been the most disgusting task I had throughout the war.

Two days later we were moving on once more, this time not on the road but across the desert to Benghasi. We now travelled with two spotters; these were put on the front mudguards, one facing forward and one backwards, an extremely uncomfortable duty but a very necessary one. One of our spotters was unique; he was a Taffy. If he tapped the windscreen and dropped off the vehicle, you knew that you still had two or maybe even three minutes to get off the wagon, run twenty or thirty yards and lie down. He was reckoned to be able to smell German aircraft. How glad we were to have him on our wagon!

We passed through Benghasi and once again pulled up for the night in our usual formation, well spread out around the cookhouse. This trip, so far as air attack was concerned, was completely uneventful. On our way up the desert we had bypassed Benghasi to get to Beda Fomm. Now that we had backtracked to be on the 'safe' side of Benghasi, we felt a little more secure. This feeling was to be dispelled the next morning. After a breakfast of tinned Australian sausages (which, incidentally, I happened to like very much), our section officer, Lieutenant Young, got us together and informed us that we were off on detachment.

The two Morris Commercials were loaded with supplies to last us for about a week. We had a good supply of demolition materials and ammo, and water. So off we went once again into the desert. While we were travelling, I was thinking to myself that, of the six of us who had been sent to join this squadron, I was the only one in this section. So my pals were being left behind me.

Once again we passed through Benghasi and on to Beda Fomm, which still looked a sorry sight, and, after motoring for about another hour, we stopped for the night with our officer still insisting that the wagons be well dispersed. After we had eaten, we were told that in the morning we would be contacting the Northumberland Fusiliers, a machine-gun unit who were actually occupying front-line positions. Our task was not yet known to our officer.

It was on this evening that I first encountered the Aussies. What a great bunch of blokes they were. A wagon came over the horizon and was approaching us at a very fast rate with a great cloud of dust behind it. We reached for our weapons, bearing in mind that the front line was very close. It soon became clear that this must be a friendly vehicle, because the enemy would surely approach us more cautiously, and so it turned out. They were Aussies of the 2nd Australian Infantry Brigade – and could they use our fire?

They set about making themselves a meal and enlightened us to the fact that up front were the Aussies, the NFs, the Rifle Brigade and very little else. I remember this conversation vividly because they also told us that the Artillery had been withdrawn and that they hadn't seen a tank for days. The Lieutenant questioned these lads very closely and I think he too came to the conclusion that they knew what they were talking about. It would appear that the Australian officers kept their men thoroughly informed of what was happening around them. However, after they had eaten, they wished us luck and took off to rejoin their unit. We all then sat discussing what the Aussies had told us before turning in for the night.

In the morning we talked again about what the Aussies had said. After we had eaten once more, we took off across the desert, where to exactly we were not told, but with the sun on our backs we were obviously heading west towards the front. This Lieutenant Young was well liked by the section, who all seemed to have great confidence in him. This in itself was very reassuring – to me, anyway – because being a newcomer to the squadron I hardly knew anybody at all.

We arrived at the position occupied by the Northumberland Fusiliers' rear echelon and Lieutenant Young was soon having a chat with some of the NF officers. We, meanwhile, were taken across to the cookhouse wagon and given a dixie of meat and veg stew (the inevitable McConachie's) and a tin of pineapple between two. Brewing up followed, and we were sitting on the deck drinking our tea when our officer returned. He sat down with us and had a mug of tea and then told us what we were about to do. As he began to talk, we heard a sharp crackling of small arms fire. It only lasted for a minute or two, but I do remember we were all up on our feet very quickly indeed. This was the first firing on the ground that we had heard and it made us realise that the enemy weren't too far away. Resuming his chat with us, the Lieutenant told us that we were to travel back about fifteen miles to a wadi that had been mined, and that our task was to lift these mines because the NFs would have to travel through the wadi in the event of a retreat.

Retreat? What was he on about? We hadn't come here to retreat! Events were to prove how right he was. We clambered aboard our two trucks and we were soon rattling once more across the desert, maintaining our fifty or sixty yards between vehicles. This trip was not to be devoid of incident because the Lieutenant's truck, being the leading vehicle, suddenly came to a halt and they dismounted very rapidly. So we simply followed suit and could plainly hear aircraft approaching.

One of the lads suddenly stood up and yelled out, 'It's OK, it's only a Lysander!' (This was a light aircraft used by the RAF for observation purposes.)

This aircraft was flying very low across our path and behind us; it made a turn to head straight for us and by now we were on our feet and giving it a wave. As it passed we could see very plainly that it was not a Lysander but a Fieseler Storch, with very German markings. These planes are similar, so I suppose our mistake can he forgiven. Suddenly this plane up ahead did a turn and was heading back towards us. As he passed us, the pilot gave us a wave. He must have been a very cool customer indeed, or was he just taking the mickey?

We resumed our journey without any further incident and reached our wadi by about 4 p.m. The wadi itself was like a gorge with a thirty-foot wide track running through it. The high ground extended from either side of the wadi for about a mile or so. I couldn't understand why it was necessary to lift the mines in the wadi when, by travelling a mile or so either side of the high ground, it was possible to go round it. The Lieutenant enlightened me on that one. It seemed that at each end of the high ground there were very extensive minefields stretching out into the desert. The rest of the squadron hadn't been idle. We started to sort the mines out immediately and worked on until about 8 p.m. when we knocked off, had a meal and settled down in our bivvies for the night. The job took us another two days before our officer was satisfied that the place was clean and therefore safe for vehicles to use it freely once again.

Our next port of call was to be Benghasi, where our officer had to report to somebody for further orders. It was also an opportunity to get to a supply dump and replenish our dwindling stock. It was that day, while we were in Benghasi, that it became noticeable that there was a large amount of traffic on the road, all of which was heading due east.

On his return, our officer gathered us around him and gave us the 'griff', which is Army talk for news. It appears that there was a 'flap' on. It was thought that the enemy were preparing to attack and our next job would be to get to the Benghasi escarpment and prepare charges to blow a few large lumps out of it. So once again we set off, this time not too far, because the escarpment was just outside the town. By now there was a constant stream of traffic leaving Benghasi and of course using the escarpment to continue along the coast road. This made our job that much more difficult. However, the Lieutenant chose two U-turns where we were to place our charges, linking them up so that they would both blow at once.

While we were working on these charges, the traffic leaving the town was undergoing frequent air attacks. Being up on the escarpment gave us a bird's-eye view of all that was going on.

Quite a number of vehicles were hit and we saw the Bofors guns down on the side of the road shoot two Jerry aircraft out of the sky. One of these was dive-bombing the vehicles and, while in his dive, the Bofors shot his tail right off. He just kept straight on, diving right into the deck amid a terrific explosion. That pilot didn't feel a thing.

By now it was about 5 p.m. and, leaving a sapper by the exploder box, we returned to our two vehicles at the top of the escarpment. We felt that a bite to eat wouldn't come amiss, as we had worked pretty hard during this particular day. After we had eaten, we were looking across to Benghasi and could see and hear that there was a little fighting going on in the town. It would seem that some sort of rearguard was putting up some resistance.

The traffic now leaving the town was getting thinner and thinner, so we knew that the order to blow the road would not be too long in coming. It was at this time that a truck arrived at the top of the escarpment with a Humber staff car behind it and came straight over to our two wagons. When they came to a halt, the Lieutenant walked over to the car as an officer with a red band round his hat got out. He was not a redcap but some sort of staff officer. They had a short conversation and then the officer returned to his staff car and sped off. I remember thinking that he wasn't the last to leave Benghasi, because there was still a trickle of traffic coming towards us from the town. The Lieutenant told us to hold ourselves in readiness to leave because we had been ordered to blow the road in one hour's time. It was to be a very long hour, because now there was only the occasional truck grinding its way up the escarpment. In fact, when the hour was up, there were still a few stragglers to be seen heading in our direction and I take my hat off to Lieutenant Young for not blowing the road for a further fifteen minutes. When we did actually blow the road, though, there were still British vehicles heading our way; I suppose orders are orders and our officer had done as much as he could in extending the time.

We packed our gear away on the trucks and once more took off, heading back to God knows where. Once out on to the desert again, it was quite an eye-opener to see all these trucks wildly heading in the same direction. I wondered where the rest of the squadron was, as we hadn't set eyes on any of them for about a fortnight. We kept going until 2 or 3 a.m., before pulling up for some sleep. We could see to the far south of us many flashes and bangs, but I was so darn tired that I soon dropped off into a deep sleep. I was woken by one of my mates, who had prepared a brew and put my mug, nicely filled, in my hand. Then I was struck by how quiet it was. There was no movement of traffic, no noise of any action anywhere. It was almost uncanny; in fact, the only two vehicles in sight were our own.

Breakfast was prepared, rather hurriedly, but at least it was my favourite – Aussie sausages. With another mug of tea, they went down a real treat. After we had all finished eating, we were told that we were heading for a place called El Mechili. We were expected to reach this place in about three hours, all being well. There was still nothing to be seen in any direction. It seemed very strange, motoring away with nothing at all about. Eventually, in the distance, straight ahead of us, we could see a large number of vehicles, and when we got to within about a mile of them we suddenly realised that we were being fired upon. We pulled up and made a quick exit over the side of the trucks and lay down. The firing stopped; the Lieutenant got into the driving seat of his truck and called to our driver to do likewise. He then kept flashing his headlights and told our driver to do the same. We all then climbed aboard and proceeded very slowly forward. There was no more firing at us, and we were able to approach the forward vehicles of whoever it was that had welcomed us with gunfire.

We were greeted by soldiers of an Indian regiment who were part of a perimeter defensive line, thrown around what appeared, at a guess, to be about three or four hundred vehicles. These were the boys who had been firing at us. Inside the perimeter, it was a bit of a shambles, a mixture of all sorts of odds and sods. We were told where to park our trucks by two redcaps – so it would appear that there was some sort of order here, after all. We were located alongside a signals unit, of which I was to learn a great deal later.

Late in the afternoon there was an almighty rush for cover, because we came under shell fire. A fair number of casualties ensued from this, both in men and vehicles. One thing that was plain to us was that we had no artillery, because we neither heard nor saw any return fire. The shelling lasted for about half an hour and shortly afterwards the Lieutenant came over to us and instructed us to grab our small packs and arms, as we had been detailed to join the perimeter defences. This news was not received with any joy at all. It was now about 5 p.m., we had slept for only about five or six hours and we hadn't eaten since breakfast.

Our post was situated on a slight rise about half a mile from the mass of vehicles. It was a weapon pit about four feet deep and it wasn't possible to go deeper because the bottom was solid rock. We had relieved three men who were from the RASC and who had been in the pit all day. They told us that they had seen absolutely nothing. The pits on either side of us were about fifteen yards away. So we sat in the pit, with one man on watch, and waited. We could see everything straight ahead for about four to five hundred yards. Beyond that the ground dropped away; this was known to us old soldiers as 'dead ground'. With nothing much to do, one could only sit and think. First and foremost in my mind was what was going to happen to us – and would we have a chance to get out of this place? I had received no news from home for over three months. I just hoped that my family and my girlfriend and her family were safe and well.

Suddenly we were shaken out of our reverie by a command shouted from pit to pit. 'Fix bayonets!' My heart fell out of the bottom of my boots. It was about 6 p.m. and suddenly we could hear engines and, from the dead ground ahead, we could see dust rising into the air. Then I can remember thinking what a strange sight, for there, right in front of us, came a large number of motor bikes and sidecars. Suddenly, we could see fire coming from the sidecars, which had machine guns mounted on them. We opened up on them alongside. Taffy was using a Boyes anti-tank rifle. We were obtaining hits right away; they were coming off those bikes like ninepins. After only about ten minutes or so, some of them turned about to break off the engagement, but they were still being hit. After the few survivors had disappeared from view and the dust had settled, the silence that followed was uncanny.

About ten minutes later, we saw three ambulances of the

RAMC going out to pick up the enemy wounded who, it transpired, were Italian. I was jubilant, as it was the very first bit of face-to-face action I had taken part in and, for our side, it had turned out extremely well.

We stood to through the night, but there was no further activity at all. I wondered how far away the Italians were, beyond that dead ground. Rations were brought round to us with a welcome brew-up. After about another hour in the pit, we were relieved by some members of the tank corps, who had obviously lost there tanks. They ribbed us a lot about the previous night's activities, which we took in good part, because we were not at all sorry to get out of that pit.

Returning to our wagon, we just climbed in the back, stretched out and were soon enjoying a good sleep. This was not to last long. By a sudden crashing and banging we were aroused, to find that we were being shelled. There was a great deal of confusion, with everybody trying to find some sort of cover. We could see tanks in the distance, the flashes from their guns plainly visible. They were circling us and I was struck that it was just like cowboys and Indians.

This went on for about an hour until we suddenly got the word that it was every man for himself. I've never seen such confusion. Wagons were taking off all over the place, mainly heading east and all probably trying to head for Cairo. Great clouds of dust filled the air as all these wagons got on the move. Beside us, our officers' wagon, with the Sergeant, Corporal and four of our sappers, also went off, following the main stream.

The shelling had ceased and we were standing by our wagon. We now consisted of a lance corporal and four sappers. A quick chat among us and we agreed that we didn't give much hope for that lot who were heading east, because the Jerry tanks would probably chop them up. So we decided that we would head west for a few miles, then turn south into the desert, a bit deeper, and then turn off east. It was a pretty safe bet that the Jerries would go after the larger body of traffic. So we piled on to the truck and set off in the opposite direction to the main stream.

After we had gone a couple of miles, we came under some fire. Where it was coming from we could not see, but we could see their bullets pinging into the sand alongside us. This firing continued for about a minute and then ceased. It was then that we realised that we were on our own; there was no other vehicle heading in our direction, so maybe our move might be going to pay off.

We continued travelling for about half an hour and were beginning to feel that our chances were getting better by the minute, when all of a sudden, dead ahead, there appeared a dirty great tank. We came to a sharp halt and we all got off the truck, holding our rifles. The tank came up to us sideways on and stopped about thirty yards from us. Its gun traversed to point at us and it fired. We all dropped to the ground and when we looked up a very young-looking officer had climbed out of the tank and was covering us with his revolver.

Walking towards us he said in perfect English, 'You are my prisoners; for you the war is over.'

He called out something in German and two of his men climbed out of the tank; both of them had revolvers and they went over to our truck. The officer signalled to us to follow them, so there we all were, standing around our truck. He said something to one of the tank crew, who started to rummage about in our truck. The crewman found a carton of Craven A ciggies and a crate of Carnation milk. What followed astounded me: the German officer had his crewman open them up. He then said to us, 'I think it fair to share them out between us all, is that not so?'

That was exactly what he proceeded to do. After this little episode was over, he waved his weapon in our direction and said, 'I would like you to know that I fired well above your heads.' He was a remarkable man.

He then told us to get back on to our truck and follow his tank, and it was here that the comedy started. We were all on our truck and it just would not start; there followed much talk among the Germans. Then we were told to get off the vehicle and to climb up on to the back of the tank behind the turret. There we were, sitting with our backs to the turret, when one of the Germans began fastening a rope to the side of the tank. He then threw it across us to one of his comrades on the other side of the tank, who proceeded to fasten the other end of the rope. The rope now went more or less across our middles.

Their officer then came round to the back of the tank and said, 'Please to understand, I have not tied you up. This rope is to help you not to fall off. I must now destroy your vehicle.'

He did just that – just one round reduced it to a smouldering wreck.

The tank started to rattle along and within a minute or so we were covered from head to toe with a thick layer of choking dust. It was a lousy ride. Eventually the journey came to an end. We were stopped alongside a large number of German vehicles, clustered by the main coast road. We were untied and were trying to get all the dust from our face and hair when the German tank officer came up to us and said, 'Not very nice for you with the dust, but in Germany it will be good.' He saluted us and left. I remember thinking that this one had behaved like a real gentleman towards us. We were then escorted by a young German soldier to a white house that stood on the side of the road.

He took us into a courtyard of the house and gestured towards a large tub full of water and mimed washing, for which we were very grateful. We promptly took advantage of this. How lovely it felt to get rid of that dust from our hair and faces! After we had cleaned up, the Jerry took us back to where all the German vehicles were and we were given a drink of coffee and some German bread, which was wrapped in tin foil. It seemed to me to be quite fresh and was, I know, very much appreciated at the time.

At this moment, a flight of German planes went past overhead and I thought how strange it was that I could not recall having seen a British plane since leaving Mersah Matruh. They were conspicuous by their absence. Our Jerry guard now signalled to us to get moving, indicating the direction by using his rifle. He took us about a couple of hundred yards to a small wagon and, after some talk with the Jerries there, he indicated that we had to climb aboard. Our sentry climbed into the back with us and the vehicle took off. We wondered what was in store for us now.

After about an hour, we could see that we were on the outskirts of Derna, and before actually entering the town we came to a makeshift prison camp. It consisted merely of barbed wire enclosing a large portion of desert. But we did note that all the guards were Italian. There were no formalities of any sort; they simply opened the front gates and gestured us in and that was it. One thing that did strike me, though, was that there appeared to be as many guards as there were prisoners. Inside there must have been several hundred prisoners, who I thought were looking extremely scruffy. I then realised that I myself was looking exactly the same. On reflection, I supposed that they had all undergone something similar to us, so in a way, were entitled to look as they did.

On talking to some of the inmates, I discovered that some had been 'in the bag' for a week. They said that the Italians brought water to the camp each morning and issued one can of captured McConachie's to each prisoner and an Italian army biscuit. This biscuit was a real gem. It was about five inches square and three eighths of an inch thick and was as hard as iron.

Toilet facilities were non-existent. The prisoners themselves had designated an area in one corner of the camp for passing water; for anything else you went up to the guard on the gate and said, '*gabinetto*'. He would call another guard, of whom there was an abundance, who accompanied you a few yards into the desert, allowed you to complete your mission and walked you back through the gate. Not a very pleasant arrangement, but I suppose at that time, having only been captured a short while, there wasn't a great deal else that the prisoners could do.

I was captured with what I stood up in, which consisted of shirt, shorts, greatcoat and plimsolls. The reason for the plimsolls was that, after travelling through the night to El Mechili, and then through our little action on the following night, my feet were barking. When we had been stood down and returned to our truck, I had put them on to ease my feet. I was still in possession of my small pack, which the Jerries who captured us, after looking in it, had allowed me to keep. In that I had a towel, soap, shaving tackle, two tins of Carnation milk and some Craven A ciggies. So my assets were very few.

After a few days in this place, early one morning we saw five large Fiat wagons, each with an equally large trailer, pull up outside the gates. We were off once more. No indication was given as to our destination. It was to be a journey that we would all remember very well. We were stuffed aboard these vehicles, about fifty men in each one. It was an absolute crush, with very little room to move, and many stops had to be made because some among us were suffering with gippy tummies. At one stop we were all made to dismount and all those who were really ill were put into one wagon. It was because we were making too many stops and the journey was taking too long.

At long last we could see the town of Benghasi appearing up ahead. We were visiting it again in very different circumstances. On our arrival at the camp, which appeared to be some sort of empty warehouse, we were given a tin of Italian army meat and one of their floor tiles – in other words, a biscuit. This tinned meat was about one third of the size of a tin of our bully and it was quite some time before we twigged that it tasted sweet because it was horse meat. At this camp each day we had German wagons arriving to load up prisoners and take them down to the docks to unload the small freighters that were slipping across the Mediterranean. The thing about this camp that stays in my mind is the sleeping arrangements that were arranged for us. They consisted of sweet Fanny Adams. There was the concrete floor, so get your head down!

Chapter Four

I do remember that, during our stay in this camp at Benghasi, we received regular visits from the RAF, who came mainly to have a go at the docks. It was nice to know that they were still in business. We had been in this camp for about three weeks, and were really beginning to feel a bit down in the dumps, when once again the Fiat wagons arrived and we were loaded up and off once more.

We were in for the longest run of the lot this time because the final destination turned out to be Tripoli. The trip itself was absolute hell. On arrival we must have looked a really filthy, scruffy, decadent bunch, because that's just what we were. We were put on a train that puffed its way to a place called Sabratha, which was a prison camp that wasn't quite as good as Benghasi. It was a terrible place. We spent several weeks in this camp and were not at all sorry to leave it. Once again it was into the old cattle trucks and back to the station in Tripoli. We were then marched down to the docks, where we boarded a small freighter. We went straight into the holds and once we were all down below a tarpaulin was put over the entrance.

Down here it was as black as Newgate's knocker and, with the number of us down there, it soon became unbearably hot. After a while, an officer among us went up the steps and pulled the tarpaulin down. Up top there was an immediate uproar, with the sentry shouting at the top of his lungs. Eventually, one of the ship's officers came to the entrance of the hold and had a chat with our officer. What transpired was that if we returned the tarpaulin the entrance would be left uncovered and we could go to the ship's latrine two at a time, under guard. The first few up to the toilets came back with the news that the guards were wearing life jackets and had their boots slung around their necks. It seems they had the greatest respect for the Royal Navy. It didn't augur well for our chances, though, down there in the hold. As it happened, the trip was uneventful and after a couple of days we docked in Bari.

We were marched through the town and gazed upon as if we had arrived from another planet. We must have presented a pretty awful sight to the local population, because by now we were a decidedly dirty, sorry-looking bunch. Once more we arrived at a railway station where, before boarding the train, we were all given a ladle of oily water that they called '*zuppa*' or, to us, soup. I did find three or four pieces of macaroni in mine and some of the lads said that I had got hold of a really thick ladle. They also gave each of us a small bread roll, which was very welcome.

On the train I have no recollection of the trip because I know that I fell asleep shortly after getting on board. I do, however, remember arriving in Naples and being kept on board the train all through the night, which seemed interminable because, having slept nearly all day, I wasn't at all tired.

The following morning, after some shunting around, we were once again on the move, where we knew not. However, this trip was to be a very short one and we soon pulled in to a station displaying the name of Capua. Amid a great deal of Italian shouting we were marshalled outside the station, where we fell in to three ranks and an Italian officer began a head count. This proved to be an extremely difficult operation for him because they kept arriving at a different total. We were to become very used to this little pantomime. After a time they seemed to be satisfied with the figures and we marched off to our next camp with about a battalion of Italian soldiers guarding us.

This camp, we discovered, was a transit camp. It was quite a large place and there must have been a couple of thousand prisoners in it. It was here that I saw my first volcano because we could plainly see Vesuvius, with a vapour rising from its crater.

The next morning we new arrivals were treated to the attentions of the camp barber. He robbed all of us of every hair we had on our heads. Then, pure bliss, we were marched off for a shower. What an uproar there was when the guards tried to get us to come out. They won in the end by simply turning off the water. It was a great feeling to be clean once more.

It was in Capua that I was to become acquainted with the

good works of the British Red Cross Society. Shortly after our arrival, we were issued with Red Cross parcels; it was a distribution of one parcel between two men. The tinned food that was unpacked was a sight for sore eyes. We were so very grateful for this parcel of food because we were beginning to realise that what we were being given by the Italians would amount to about a fifth or sixth of our normal diet. We were supposed to be given the normal rations of an Italian soldier.

First thing in the morning we were given coffee, which was generally thought to be made with burnt acorns; with this we received a small bread roll. The weight of this, I believe, was about two hundred grams, or about three ounces. This piece of bread was our day's ration. We would eat a small piece with our coffee and then try to save a piece to eat with our two ladles of soup. We had one ladle of this soup at midday and one at about 5.30 p.m. It was invariably a pink colour – this I suppose indicated the presence of some tomato purée. It was about ninety per cent liquid and the remainder consisted of either rice or macaroni. Once, I drained off the liquid just to see how much solid there was in it – it was just enough to fill one spoon.

Once a week we had an issue of cheese. The room orderlies would go to the cookhouse to collect this and it was issued by weight, according to the number of men in the hut. Once in the hut of, say, sixty prisoners, the men would usually split into six groups. The cheese would then be cut into six portions and then one man from each group would cut the cards to see who had first choice of the pieces of cheese. The same procedure would often be followed by the group. It was a very considerable insight into how important the fair sharing of food had become, especially when the final outcome of all this procedure was a piece of cheese about the size of an Oxo cube.

One day, for some reason or other, the authorities had run out of sugar, so there was nothing to put in the coffee. Later in the day we were issued with some oranges in lieu of the sugar. We were supplied with sufficient oranges for a distribution of one orange between five men. It was becoming increasingly obvious to us that the most important thing in our life behind barbed wire was going to be food.

After about two months in this place, during which time our hair had grown to a half-inch stubble, we were told that we would be moving on to another camp. It was once again a march to the station and on to a train, our destination again unknown. This journey took four days; we spent more time at a standstill in sidings than we did travelling. All we could figure out was that we were going in a northerly direction. I was beginning to think that the Italians were really afraid of us, even though they were the guards and we were the prisoners. I thought this because I remembered seeing thousands and thousands of Italian prisoners in the desert, being shepherded along by a couple of Bren gun-carriers. We once again seemed to have almost as many guards as prisoners. We had been given two tins of Italian horsemeat and two of their famous biscuits as rations for the journey. Thank God for the bit of food we had with us from our Red Cross parcels. What a life-saver they were!

When we finally came to a halt, we were at a place called Bolzano. This was in the north of Italy. When we left the station and were on the march to our next camp, I was struck by the number of Germans there were about.

I remember this march very well; it was to last for about an hour and a half. It was a very hot day indeed. I was very tired and extremely thirsty. Finally we came to a place called Prato all'Isarco, our new camp. Until our arrival, this place had been empty. It was in a very narrow valley, high mountains all around us, and running through the town was a river. We discovered that this was the River Isarco. There were also a road and a railway. The camp was situated right alongside the road with the river and railway beyond.

On entering the camp, we were all paraded while the Camp Commandant harangued us about our behaviour in camp: we were to obey orders, we were to obey the guards, we were to obey the carabinieri who would be patrolling the camp on the inside by day and by night. He went on for a considerable time and I can remember praying for him to shut up so that I could get a drink.

Eventually the Italian colonel's lecture came to an end and we were allocated our huts and our bunks. There was quite a queue at the tap for a drink of water.

A word about the camp: it was, of course, surrounded, by the usual barbed wire, but with a difference. This wire had hundreds of tin cans hanging inside the meshes. I suppose the thinking was that anyone attempting an escape through the wire would kick up quite a racket. Sound logic, but it did have a drawback because, whenever there was a good breeze (which was quite often considering the position of the camp), there was always this tinkling of the cans.

Our numbers in this camp were about 400, and very soon all sorts of activities were organised to occupy our time and our minds. I can remember the camp choir that used to sing in one corner of the camp down by the road every Sunday evening. After a short while they had a fairly large audience of local villagers standing outside the wire and applauding their efforts. This activity was soon stopped and they had to do their singing in one of the huts. We even had our own kind of Olympics, with the lads splitting into teams with the most unlikely names. I can recall one team called itself the Mechili Harriers. All the running and jumping and so on was generously applauded by the local population. The Aussies figured prominently among the winners. Although the food in this camp was on a par with that which we had received at Capua, we were a lot better off now because we were getting a Red Cross parcel per man per week, plus a Red Cross issue of cigarettes.

The huts here were laid out in two rows, end to end. As it was not permitted to smoke in the huts, we had an arrangement that the man in the end bed by the door would give warning if a carabinieri was about to enter the hut. My bed was on the end. One day we were in the hut when I spotted a carabinieri approaching, I gave a whistle and shouted 'Fags out', then forgot all about it. At the following morning's roll call it was obvious that something was up. All the Italian officers were present, from the Colonel down. The Colonel had no English so he first shouted out in Italian to one of his officers, who then did the translation. It appeared that a terrible crime had been committed by one of us. Somebody had insulted the carabinieri by whistling at him. This, we were told, would not be tolerated and unless the guilty party owned up there would be no further issues of Red Cross parcels.

I couldn't let that happen, so I took a pace forward. Two guards marched me up to the officers and the Colonel went on at me for about two minutes – with me not understanding a word. Once he had stopped, the interpreter told me that the Colonel had said that I was a very bad soldier and must go to prison.

The lock-up was located in the top left-hand corridor of the camp, adjacent to the latrines. On the far side of the lock-up were the admin buildings. All I was permitted to take into the jail was my blanket, washing gear and a dixie.

Now, the Aussies were gamblers. They used to play a game called 'three up'. This consisted of placing three coins on the palm of the hand and tossing them in the air; bets would be struck on how they landed. The currency used was cigarettes. This game always took place by the side of the latrines, every day after the evening soup. When I and another prisoner who was unknown to me were led out under guard for our last visit of the day to the latrine, we had to pass by the Aussies, hard at it on their gambling. Once inside the latrine, the first thing we did was to grab the cigarettes and matches that were passed through the window by the Aussies. I've said before and I'll always say that the Aussies took some beating. They were great. Good on yer, cobbers!

Our soup was brought to the jail by one of the cooks and we always got a dixie full. It amounted to double rations, but of course we had no Red Cross parcel. It seemed strange being sent to jail without any sort of trial and two months were to pass by before I was released. Our cell doors were opened one day and we were taken outside into the courtyard of the jail. There awaiting us was the Italian interpreter, who said to us, 'Today is the Colonel's birthday, you are free.' They certainly had some strange ways.

It was about a week after my release that the carabinieri came looking for me. I wondered what I was in for now. I was escorted to the admin building, where the interpreter was waiting for me, and I was then taken up to the Colonel's office. He was seated behind his desk. I came to attention and saluted him. He then stood up, returned my salute and sat down again. On his desk was a parcel about a foot or so long and six inches square. Through the interpreter, he said that the parcel was addressed to me and he wanted to know what was in it. I replied that I had no idea what was in it. He then asked who had sent it. I again replied that I had no idea. They talked among themselves for a minute or so, then the interpreter told me that I was to open it. This I did, to reveal 200 John Player's Navy Cut cigarettes and a card that simply said: 'From Dad.'

It was the first parcel that had ever been received at the camp. The Colonel seemed intrigued by the fact that although I was a prisoner I could receive such bounty from my family. I then offered them both a cigarette, which they accepted. I was thinking that to give two to take 198 was better than having them confiscated. They lit their cigarettes and the interpreter told me that they were very good. I was then dismissed and the guard returned me to the compound.

There was much jubilation in the hut when I returned with my parcel – now they could all live in hopes and soon the air was thick with smoke. Very soon after getting my parcel, many of the other lads started to receive them.

Day after day, throughout all of our time in the camp, we would try our luck at asking our jailers for various different items: wood for our fires, material to repair our boots, or even an extra piece of bread. The answer was the same each day: *domani, sempre domani* (tomorrow, always tomorrow).

Some time later, a few of the lads used their ingenuity and made us a camp crest complete with our camp motto, which was of course: Always tomorrow and we're in the s—t.

Years later, after the war and at the inauguration of our Annual Reunion, a very nice mahogany copy of the crest was made, complete with motto. It hung in the Union Jack Club for years, a testament to humour in adversity.

I mentioned earlier that we had a good view of the railway from the camp. We could see numerous trains heading through the Brenner Pass loaded with German tanks and vehicles, heading no doubt for the desert. We were always wondering how things were going out there because these were still early days for us as prisoners and news for us was scarce.

The first mail was now beginning to arrive in the camp. I was soon to receive some both from my parents and my girlfriend. We were allowed one letter and one postcard every month, so I sent these turn about to my parents and my girl.

One day a party of a dozen of us were taken outside the camp and marched some distance up the road until we came to a wagon with two civilians. These people were woodcutters, and we were taken into the woods at the side of the road and given to understand that our job was to carry the timber, as it was cut into suitable lengths, and load it on the wagon. We had two guards, which was very unusual. Going by previous moves outside camp, we should have had about ten. However, after about a couple of hours, the guards, one of whom was where the cutting was going on, the other by the wagon, seemed to me to be very relaxed. They were actually both sitting down. So, after a trip down to the wagon with a length of timber on my shoulder, I thought to myself that, when we were about halfway back, neither guard could see us. Accordingly, I took off into the woods and up the side of the mountain.

It was pure impulse. I hadn't even prepared myself for an escape. I had no food and no idea in which direction to take off. It was, I suppose, a pretty stupid thing to do, all things considered. Anyway, I kept going for a couple of hours, climbing all the time, until I came out of the thick trees into more open ground. Looking back and down, I could see the village and the camp. I reckoned that they were about four or five kilometres away, so I pressed on, simply putting distance between me and the camp. As I walked on around the mountain, the village soon went from view. I kept going until dusk and then started to look for a sheltered spot where I could hole up for the night. I spent a very miserable night; it was very cold and I had very little sleep.

As soon as it was light I started walking again; at least I felt a little warmer. Up to now I had not encountered a living soul and all I could hear was birdsong here and there. I kept going for the whole of the second day. As evening approached, I was beginning to realise that I couldn't keep going like this without food of some sort. As night fell, I found a sheltered spot and tried to settle down for some sleep. I do remember that I slept for about four hours and woke up shivering.

I realised that I would have to start coming down lower from the mountain if I was somehow going to find something to eat. It was still quite dark so there was not much point in making a move just yet. As dawn broke I started to descend the mountain, still hoping I was walking away from the camp. I could suddenly see some houses on a bend in the road so I sat down to watch, to see if there was any activity going on down there. Then I had a feeling that I was being watched. I got up and looked around me and there, standing about thirty yards away, was a man wearing knee breeches and long socks, a leather coat and a kind of Tyrolean hat. The worst part was the fact that he had a shotgun trained on me and, amazingly, he was smiling at me. He gestured with the gun that I was to move off downward and he fell in right behind me. He walked me right down to the road and gestured toward the houses, which were about a couple of hundred yards up the road. We passed three or four of these houses and then he turned towards a building, that was, to me, self-explanatory. It had a sign outside that said 'Carabinieri'. I was back in the bag.

They knew who I was and where I had come from; I expect some sort of alarm had been passed along. I was put in a room with a carabinieri as a guard. With a little pantomime I was able to get him to understand that I was starving. He nodded his head and yelled out something through the door. A few minutes later, in came one of his colleagues with some bread, cheese and some grapes. I thanked them, and then showed them how hungry I was, as the food vanished very quickly. I was very grateful to them. After a couple of hours, a wagon arrived with a driver and three guards to escort me back the camp. Once we returned I was immediately put in a cell in the camp jail. I do remember, though, that as I was marched in there was a round of applause from the lads who had seen my arrival. This seemed to anger the guards and I was much prodded by rifles.

I was in the jail for over a week before I was brought before the Colonel, who very kindly told me that I was to serve twenty-eight days in the jail. It turned out that I actually did thirty-two days. The Italians had a strange way of doing things! The routine in jail was exactly the same as before. The cookhouse provided us with two ladles of whatever was on the menu and our evening trip to the latrine, then provided us with a smoke during the following day. Upon my release into the camp, I had to report to the admin building twice a day, at 11 a.m. and 3 p.m., where my attendance was noted in a book, and then I had to wait until their sergeant could find an officer to add his signature to the entry. They seemed determined to keep a close eye on me.

We were told on roll call one day that we would be leaving this camp the following morning. We were going to a 'permanent camp', where the facilities were much better for us, as this was only a transit camp – so they said.

Early the next day we could be seen retracing our steps back on the road to Bolzano station and we were once again boarding a train. This trip took us two days; we arrived at our destination at a town called Sulmona at about 9 p.m. We trekked for an hour or so before we came to the camp, by which time it was getting quite dark. We had the usual search of our few belongings and our persons. We then went in file into another large room, where we were handed a calico sack and shown a huge pile of straw; so we proceeded to fill our sacks. We were then taken to our huts and allocated a bed and thankfully got our heads down.

This was a very large camp indeed. It had a sergeants' compound, an officers' compound, another full of Yugoslavians and three compounds of other ranks. I discovered that I was in No. 3 compound. In this we had all ranks of the Army, Navy and RAF. The inmates had got things very well organised. There were all sorts of activities going on. They had a handball league, a cricket league, a compound cribbage tournament, a theatre and they also held elections to appoint a mayor of the compound. This last was an absolute riot because each candidate would hold election meetings and the promises they would give you if you would give them your vote were the funniest things I ever encountered as a prisoner.

I was first put into hut No. 64. This was at the top of the compound, right by the wall that separated us from the officers' compound. The very first morning I was to discover that our communication with the officers was on a regular basis, because just outside the entrance to my hut there came two lads from the Rifle Brigade, who removed a couple of bricks from the wall, whistled through, and we were soon in conversation with someone on the other side. The hut immediately over the wall housed the officers' batmen, who relayed the messages. The two lads from the Rifle Brigade (Sidney 'Clicker' Clarke and Bobby Dodge) were later to become my cellmates.

One day, we had a new Italian officer come in to take the morning roll call. After the usual count and recount, and earnest chat with his minions, he was satisfied that we were all there. He then commenced to address us as follows: 'You willa cutta da air, trimma da beard and sweepa da compound.' This was greeted with a great howl of laughter from the prisoners and he went absolutely berserk. Shouting and bawling in Italian, he vented his anger on his minions and then left the compound. He even forgot to dismiss us.

Chapter Five

One afternoon, about 2 p.m., we were called out on parade and immediately there was a frantic toing and froing and a hurried hiding of certain articles that were not permitted by the Italians. We were expecting a snap search. This, however, was not the reason for the parade. After we had all fallen in, the compound gates were opened and in stalked the Camp Commandant, sundry Italian officers and three or four German officers. Now this was an unusual sight! We hadn't set eyes on a German since leaving Bolzano.

The senior German began to address us in faultless English. The gist of his speech was that we had been captured on Italian territory, therefore we were imprisoned in Italy, but we could, if we so wished, volunteer to go to a camp in Germany, where we would be treated almost like civilians. The camp had all mod cons, including a cinema. We would be only four to a room and there were three meals a day. The sporting facilities included a football pitch and a gymnasium, among other things. We were to be given a form that was simply asking our trade or profession, our date of birth and our nationality. All we had to do to volunteer was to sign the form at the bottom. The forms would be returned to the compound office by midday on the following day. We were all then issued with the magic form that was going to take us to this German Shangri-La. Then we were dismissed.

On returning to our respective huts, a great deal of discussion ensued; it was generally agreed that the camp was a pipe dream and that the only really significant part of the form was where they required you to state your trade or profession. So the forms were duly filled in. There didn't appear to be a tradesman in the camp. There were road sweepers, lamplighters, billiard hall markers, kangaroo ranchers, elephant trainers, dish-washers, cricket umpires, a magician's assistant and many others I don't remember – but I do remember a great number simply said that they were unemployed. It was agreed in the compound that not one was to be signed. These forms were duly handed in on the following day. We never heard anything else about them.

In our compound we had one very unfortunate individual who was our compound interpreter – an Italian sergeant who had been born in Italy, taken to Scotland when he was seven years old and returned to Italy to visit relations just before the outbreak of war. He used to say to us in his broad Scottish accent, 'I dropped right in it, mon.'

By now my plimsolls had given up the ghost and I was walking about on a pair of sandals that I had made out of a piece of blanket. So one day I went over to the compound office to see Jock, as we called the interpreter. I asked him if I could be issued with a pair of boots; he promised to see what he could do. During the course of the next month or so, I went back to him a couple of times to see if any boots were in the offing, with no luck. The third time I saw him, again with no luck, I said to him, 'Tell me, Jock, what *have* you got in this bloody country?' He replied, 'Well, we've got grapes, we've got tomatoes.' I did eventually get issued with a pair of Italian army boots.

We had one Italian officer who regularly took roll call in our compound, whom we had nicknamed 'Sulmona Joe'. He wasn't a bad type at all. He was fanatical about football and was instrumental in getting a stretch of waste land by the side of the admin buildings turned into a football pitch – with our labour, of course. Working parties went down to the site every day and we were given shovels and a couple of wheelbarrows to help us level and clear the site. This took us two or three months. All work done on this was entirely voluntary and there was no shortage of volunteers. Once the work was completed, we started playing there right away, using big rocks for goalposts. Sulmona Joe said he was trying to get us real goalposts and one day, sure enough, there they were. He was a good type, was Joe.

The football pitch was in almost constant use. We had an inter-compound competition and eventually we staged international matches. We had a number of professional footballers among us. I can recall Jock Watson, who kept goal for St Johnstone in the Scottish League. There were the Stevens twins, who I believe played for Leeds before the war, and one of whom played for West Ham after the war. All these 'Big Matches', as we called them, were refereed by Sulmona Joe, who always got a great cheer as he took the field.

Brewing up in the compound was one of the most important activities and it was going on in all sorts of places, at all times of the day. The tea, and of course the food that we received from the Red Cross, was one of the greatest morale boosters I can think of. This fact was very apparent when the supply dried up, which was when you really needed this most – in the winter time. I don't for a moment think that the Red Cross was in any way to blame for this. It was, in all probability, a problem of transport. I remember how miserable we all were without those parcels during those bleak months.

After a couple of attempts at escape from the camp, the Italians started to pierce all the tins that were in the parcels. This infuriated us, because it meant that we would have to use the contents almost straight away to avoid them spoiling.

To return to the subject of brewing up, one of our major problems was fuel. It soon became apparent that a lot of the fuel used was coming from illegal sources. First the doors of the latrines just disappeared, then the windows. The amazing thing about this was that nobody saw these strange occurrences actually happening. Once this got started, the thing snowballed. Very shortly the huts were open to the elements because the windows had vanished. I remember the lads in hut No. 61 complaining about their roof leaking every time it rained. The Italian reply to their request for repairs was always the same, '*Domani*' (which is Italian for 'tomorrow').

After a visit by the protecting power (a group of Swiss gentlemen) and a complaint going to them about this particular roof, the Italians did indeed commence repairs, and so aided our fuel solution. One morning, some Italian workmen were brought into the compound and started to strip the roof. As each piece of timber was placed at the side of the hut, it disappeared very promptly. The Italians went spare when they realised that their timber was vanishing.

It was about this time that the Italians started to pay us. This was because our people were paying all the prisoners who were in our hands. I well remember our first pay day. We were paid on the first day of the month, for the preceding month, at the rate of one lira per day, so we should have got thirty or thirty-one lire per month. We each received one lira and, upon querying this, we were told that the rest was for our damage to the huts, etc. Fair enough, because there was certainly a great deal of damage done to the huts, but no great hardship to us because the thirty lire would buy only a couple of packets of cigarette papers.

While on the subject of cigarettes, it brings to mind those that the Italians were smoking at the time. One was called Milit. This was by far the worst cigarette in the world; it was a tube of paper, with small twigs inside. How they were made is a mystery to me, because the paper was perforated by its contents and therefore it was almost impossible to draw smoke through. The next one was called Nazionali. These were a slight improvement on Milits – very slight! The third one was called Tre Stella and these were a better cigarette and almost impossible to obtain. I expect these were more for the officer class, because they were more expensive.

In this camp, our contact with the Italians was slight. This was because of the way that the camp was laid out. Each compound had high walls all round, with only the one entrance. Regularly, of course, we would see the Italians who came in to do the roll call, held morning and evening, with the occasional snap roll call during the day. The only other visits we got from them were their sudden searches, when they would come in, select a hut, turf everybody out and proceed to turn everything in it upside down. They used to find a little contraband (i.e. something we were not allowed to have), which seemed to give the searchers much satisfaction, but they never found anything of any great importance to us; we just hid such items with more thoroughness. It did, however, take some little time to get one's belongings sorted out and restored to any kind of order.

I had been in this camp about fifteen months and was, like many of the others incarcerated there, really fed up with the whole thing. The news was of a stalemate in the desert; the Japs had attacked Pearl Harbor and the Americans had joined the conflict. We wondered how much longer it would all take before we would win the war. Strangely, it never, ever, entered our heads that we could lose.

I was in a combine of four at Sulmona. This was a method of trying to make life a little more tolerable. It did instil a feeling of togetherness and comradeship, the like of which was not to be matched anywhere. Everything that came into our possession was split four ways. This included all our parcels from home, be they clothing parcels (which always contained chocolate) or cigarette parcels, or anything else that we got hold of, however illicitly obtained. The four consisted of myself, one lad named 'Nugger' Hall, from the famous Northumberland Fusiliers, Bobby Dodge and 'Clicker' Clarke from London, the Rifle Brigade.

Many and varied were the capers that we got up to in order to make our lot a little more bearable. The most daring among us was Bobby; he was a lad who would try anything, so long as there was an outside chance of pulling it off. What's more, he succeeded more often than he failed. Nugger was his willing partner in all these escapades. Clicker was our organiser: his main activity was looking after the food side of the combine. We had some of the most unusual dishes served up by Clicker. He could take a bread roll, some currants and rolled oats from our Red Cross parcel and make some really smashing biscuits. Not quite up to McVitie's standard, maybe, but they did make a change from our usual miserable diet. It seemed to me that our combine of four would stick together throughout, come what may, but, strangely, this was not to be.

One day we were informed by the Italians that a working camp was going to be set up and that they were asking for volunteers, who had to be tradesmen with experience in the building trade. Among the four of us this caused a great deal of discussion. Nugger would have no part of it, as he was resolutely against moving. We other three were more receptive to it, mainly because we were really cheesed off with Sulmona and felt that a change of scenery wouldn't at all come amiss.

My trade was cabinet making, so I felt that I could put myself down as a carpenter. Clicker and Bob were both solicitor's clerks. Not exactly builders, any of us, but we three felt that we would all have a go at being carpenters. So we had our names included on the list of volunteers. After some three or four weeks, we were told that we had been selected and to hold ourselves in readiness for a move. This came about a fortnight later. There was a party of about one hundred of us, being marched off to the station, placed aboard a train, and bound once again we knew not whither.

It was to be a place called L'Aquila. This turned out to be the capital city of the region known as the Abruzzi. We were marched about ten kilometres from the city to a building that had very obviously been converted to a prison camp in a great hurry. Everything was makeshift and we wondered whether we had jumped out of the frying pan into the proverbial fire. After we had been allocated our sleeping quarters, which were double-decker bunk beds, and given a ladle of the usual watery soup, we were told that the Commandant would address us. So we were all trundled out on parade to meet the new Commandant.

This was a captain, whose name was Perrone. He was, we found out later, a bank manager in the city, and seemed to do this job part-time. He had two lieutenants to assist him in his task. A word about these two: the first was a very ugly character whom we called 'Più Bello' – this is Italian for 'more beautiful'. We didn't call him this to his face, of course, only among ourselves. The other, at a later date, was to be named 'Niente Più'.

The Captain told us that we would be taken out to work on some buildings that were about five kilometres distant from the camp; this was about halfway to the city. We would work a six-day week, resting on Sunday. We were to receive an extra bread ration and told that once we arrived on the site, which was totally enclosed with the usual barbed wire, we would come under civilian direction, insofar as work was concerned. The midday soup would be brought to the site; we would be searched on leaving the camp and upon our return. Any attempt at escape would result in an immediate return to Sulmona, where we would serve our sentence for escaping and thereafter remain in Sulmona for the duration.

After we were dismissed, we returned to our rooms and were soon trying to get ourselves settled in to our new quarters. We did not have a great deal of space in this place. Everything seemed so small to us, after the large camp at Sulmona – the contrast was so marked.

Angelo Marchetti, his bride Teodalinda and his parents, Amerigo and Ausilia

The author in Sulmona Camp, 1941

Angelo's mother, Ausilia Marchetti

Angelo Marchetti, 1942

Back row, Lorenzo Morelli, Jim Kerr, Sabatino Ciuffini and Alfonsina Morelli. Front row: Tom Walsh, the author and Tommy Yoxall, May 1944

One of the author's hideouts, situated between the villages of Arischia and Cansatessa Pettino in the Abruzzi

Revisiting Hut No. 64 at the Sulmona Camp in the 1970s

Other huts in the Sulmona Camp

'Clicker' Clarke and Stan Evans on the visit to the camp in the 1970s

Another view of the reunion pals' visit to the camp

The author's 'bathroom' on the lower slopes of the mountains between Arischia and Cansatessa Pettino

The window from which the author leapt when the Germans raided the village of Cansatessa Pettino

Alfonsina Morelli, wife of Giulio (the film director), who was banned from work in Cinecittà in Rome for making an anti-fascist film

Angelo, his wife Linda and the author

The author with Bettina, wife of Pasquale

Angelo's brother Alarico and his wife Serena. He was a POW in America.

Angelo and Linda in the author's garden during their visit, on their twenty-fifth wedding anniversary

*Gabriella and Carla, Angelo Marchetti's neice and daugter,
with the author at his house*

The author's family at home with the visiting Marchettis

*The author's children, Jill and Teresa
and Angelo's Marchetti's neice Gabriella and daughter Carla*

*The Sulmona former POWs' fiftieth reunion
at the Union Jack Club, Waterloo, London, 2004*

Sidney 'Clicker' Clarke and the author outside the Union Jack Club

Chapter Six

I had by now picked up quite a smattering of the language; nothing at all in the way of grammar, but many words which were to me reasonably obvious. I could not yet understand conversation, simply a word here and there. It was, to me, great fun to use the few words I knew, but even that had its drawbacks, because I would get drawn into all sorts of situations, purely because the guards were beginning to think that I could *palare Italiano* and this was far from correct.

During our first three weeks in this camp, I remember very well, we received a Red Cross parcel per man each week. This in itself was unusual. We were then marched up the road to the place of our new employment. The site was surrounded with barbed wire and had high sentry towers at all strategic points. Once inside, we could see that all the labour consisted of Italian civilians. We were allocated to our *capo*, or foremen, according to the trade that we, that is the majority of us, had invented for ourselves. To be amongst civilians again was very strange, especially enemy civilians. We wondered how they would receive us. As it turned out, in most cases we were received very well and it soon became obvious to us that the average Italian was none too keen on the war.

The buildings we were working on were all of the same design and consisted of just two floors, ground floor and first floor. After just three days working on this site, we discovered that what we were building was a barrack block. Upon our return to camp that evening, we all had a meeting and decided that we would do no more work on this site because of its military nature. This decision of ours really did put the cat among the pigeons as far as the Italians were concerned and, after the evening roll call, the Commandant arrived at the camp and had a meeting with our camp leader. It was agreed that our camp leader could write to the protecting power, the Swiss, and put our point of view on this matter.

It was to be seven weeks before this problem was solved. It appears the Swiss had got in touch with our government and they had given their permission for us to resume working. So once again we set off to our workplace to be greeted by the Italian civvies, who started to take the mickey out of us rather a lot. It appears that they had got the impression that we had gone on strike for something or other and had lost the day, then been forced to return to work, with, according to them, much loss of face. We explained to them that it wasn't quite like that. We said that when we realised that the work was of a military nature, we had to get in touch with our government to determine whether they gave their permission for us to do this type of work. This, we said, had taken several weeks and Mr Churchill had told us that this work was quite all right; he had also instructed us to hurry it up because, when our troops arrived in Italy, they would be needing somewhere to sleep. They seemed to be subdued by this and their mickey-taking came to an end.

It was the civilians who told us that one building we were working on was to become our prison camp. They said it was the first building on the right, as we entered the site. It was remarkable that the civvies had told us this piece of news and even more remarkable that it turned out to be correct. It was indeed the building that seemed to have some sort of priority given to it, because it had the most labour working on it. Eventually it was the first building completed.

We had now been working on this site for about five weeks and, in that time, we had established a certain relationship with the Italian civvies. There was much bartering going on between us. The thing they prized most was a bar of our soap. Theirs was a piece of greyish green colour – it seemed to me like a piece of pumice stone that wouldn't lather. This swapping was for food, mainly bread, which could be eaten on site and no amount of searching would find it. Of course the trade snowballed until it could almost be termed big business. Exchange values were soon established; fluctuations in this were many and varied. The market was easily manipulated by us prisoners, all agreeing that a certain item, such as a tin of coffee from a Canadian Red Cross parcel, was not to be swapped for a month. This was an item very much prized by the civvies and when we released it on the market, our price was always a little higher than previously. Our own code of discipline in these matters was consistently excellent.

We all by now had various bits of contraband hidden away around the site and this was to cause quite a storm later on. One day, we had a gang of Italian workers arrive on the site, who started to erect a fence around the first building on the right. The information the Italian civvies had given us was beginning to appear to be correct, so all the gear that we had stashed away all over the site started to be given new homes. We all made sure that it was now hidden within the confines of the new fence, to be retrieved at a later date.

We were moved into our new building about three weeks later. It had two rooms on the left as you entered the building, one used as the camp office by our camp leader, the other as our MI room. To the right were the stairs, leading to the first floor. These stairs were to feature in quite a drama at a later date. A wide central gangway then went the length of the building, at the end of which were the showers. On either side of the gangway there were partitions put up about every twenty feet. Our beds were of the double-bunk variety with the usual wooden slats to rest our bodies, with a palliasse of straw. The second building on the right became the Italian offices and living quarters.

I had now been 'in the bag' for about fifteen months and it seemed like fifteen years, but we were receiving mail from home and this was a great morale-booster. It was unfortunate that a lot of this was deleted by the censor. How we used to wonder what it was that was underneath those black lines! I did find that when you moved from one camp to another it took about three to four months for a letter to arrive, actually addressed to the new camp.

The contraband gear that had been hidden in the new building and compound was now beginning to be retrieved from the many and varied hiding places. There were bags of potatoes that had been buried and were being dug up. Holes began appearing in the plasterwork inside the building. This was not vandalism, but mainly the retrieving of money – not the camp money, which of course was worthless outside, but genuine Italian lire that had been obtained by bartering. This cash had been pushed between the bricks, prior to plastering. Each cache was carefully plotted by its owner and it wasn't uncommon to see somebody measuring up – say three foot in from the door and four foot six up – and digging out the plaster in order to once again get hold of his hoard.

After a few days of this, the place was beginning to look a bit sorry for itself and our captors were noticeably put out about it. The Commandant addressed us on the subject for about half an hour with much screaming and shouting, of which we understood not a word – it being in Italian. The interpreter in this camp was little Sergeant Guillaume. In English this was William, so naturally we dubbed him 'Bill'. His translation of the speech was much appreciated because it was much shorter. The gist of it was that we would have to pay for the damage that we had caused. We considered that this was fair enough and through our camp leader suggested to the Commandant that we would pay for the materials and carry out the repairs ourselves. For some reason this seemed to please the Commandant and this was agreed upon. It amazed me that nobody among the Italians asked us why we had done this to such a nice new building.

It was now spring and the weather was beginning to put new heart into us all; it had been a pretty hard winter. A delivery of British Army clothing had arrived at the camp through the auspices of the British Red Cross. Before any of this was permitted to be distributed, the Italians wanted to make a few additions to the clothing. When we did finally get it they had sewn a red diamond on the back of all the blouses and a similar emblem on the right knee of the trousers. After being garbed in Yugoslavian pantaloons and other sundry bits and pieces that the Italians had given us, we felt extremely well dressed. We had previously looked a very sorry bunch indeed and I suppose that was why we attended roll calls in such a sloppy manner; even when being dismissed we just broke ranks and ambled away. What the Italians thought of us we didn't know and cared even less.

With this new boost to our morale, our camp leader had a suggestion to make to us all that was very well received: he asked us to get things shipshape from now on. He was a PO from the submarine *Oswald*, sunk in the Mediterranean. We could see that this made a lot of sense and we all agreed to show the wops a thing or two.

Our falling in for roll call, our marching to and from our work, our drilling, were all to become a revelation to the Italians, with our leaders exhorting us to show the Italians what real soldiers looked like. We set to with a will, always with a feeling of superiority and, whenever possible, to rub their noses in it! This was achieved in all sorts of ways. One of the most memorable of these was the very first evening roll call we had after the new clothing was issued to us. These were generally taken by the Commandant himself after he had knocked off work at the bank. PO Kennedy and the Commandant waited while the Italians counted us two or three times to get their sums right, and the Commandant had obviously said something to Kennedy about the clothing. Kennedy raised the hem of his greatcoat and showed it to the Commandant and then raised the Commandant's coat so that he could compare the quality. The Italian's coat had no hem and it had cottons hanging from it; he didn't look at all pleased!

By now there were many prisoners in the camp who had no work, as these barracks were almost completed. Rumours, of course, were rife and there was much speculation as to what the future held for us. At least the war news was much better – things were happening in the desert and it appeared that the tide was turning. It was during this period in the camp, when the majority of prisoners were not working, that we had a newcomer to the camp. He was Sergeant Major Romain, a member of the South African Army. To everybody in the camp he was a total stranger; not a soul knew him or anything about him. We were to find out about him however – a very great deal!

The work situation was to sort itself out within two or three weeks. It appeared that the Italians had contracted our labour to two Italian building companies, one named Rotundi, the other Lorenzetti. These two firms had jobs going in the city of L'Aquila. Bob, Clicker and I were detailed to work as carpenters for Rotundi, whose enterprise was the building of the L'Aquila branch of the Bank of Roma. We marched every day to and from the job in our new battledress. We all marched to attention with

55

bags of swank and really put to shame the poor guards in their tatty uniforms.

Both these sites, like our last job, had the usual barbed wire all round and plenty of sentries. On site we would all change into our old clobber and start 'work'. First and foremost was making contact with a new bunch of civilians and establishing 'trade agreements' with them. There was a tremendous amount of bartering going on, a great deal of vino was being consumed on the site, and the lads were certainly making the most they could out of the situation in which they found themselves. Not content with their drop of vino on the job, a lot of the lads began smuggling it back into the camp in their water bottles. After a few weeks this vino was actually being bartered inside the camp among the prisoners themselves.

Saturday night soon became a party night, with of course the odd few who would overdo it and become a little too merry. I should mention that by now, in the canteen, we could actually buy (beside cigarette papers and razor blades) vino. It happened therefore that one Saturday night, in the midst of the revelry, we had a visit from the Italian orderly officer. He went absolutely spare, yelling and raving, '*Niente più, niente più!*' which meant 'no more'. This officer was for ever after called 'Tenente Niente Più', or 'Lieutenant No More'. The sale of vino in the canteen was stopped from that moment on and it never did come back.

Our camp leader, the South African, was beginning to come under some suspicion, because he was frequently missing from the camp for up to four days at a time. His excuse when challenged on these absences was that the Italians wanted him to see how other work camps were being run to help make ours more efficient. This statement was treated with a great deal of caution by everybody in the camp. It took a couple of weeks to discover that, in fact, every time he left the camp his destination was always the same: he always went to Rome.

It transpired that he was actually broadcasting anti-Allied propaganda. With this knowledge, our camp committee planned his demise. As we had no weapons to do the job, it was agreed that we would obtain a rope from the site, put it round his neck on the first-floor landing, tie the rope to the railing and throw him over the side. This would leave him dangling by the stairs, just inside our camp entrance. Having done this, we were going to report to the Italians immediately that we had a suicide for them.

All these preparations were to come to nothing. Too many people were in on the scheme and, somehow or other, the Italians got wind of it and he was whisked away. He was a very lucky man indeed, as he would certainly have died in L'Aquila prison camp.

It was a routine every morning for each group of men to sweep out their own bed space and push the sweepings out into the main gangway. This was then cleared by the barrack-room orderlies. For the disposal of this rubbish we had a large box with shafts at each corner; it was routine that at about mid-morning the room orderlies with a couple of other chaps would each take a corner of the box and carry it over to the main gate, where the sentry on the gate would call to the guardroom for a spare guard to escort the four men with the box of rubbish outside the camp to a pit that had been dug by the prisoners. The box was then upended and the four men returned to the camp. This daily, humdrum little act was to be very important to me at a later date.

Chapter Seven

By now it was July 1943 and it was a very hot summer. We knew that the Germans had been cleared out of North Africa, so our morale was running pretty high and we were all beginning to adopt a more confident attitude. As we moved into August, the news that our forces had landed in Sicily was received in the camp with much joy and anticipation. It was generally felt in the camp that the Italians would throw in the towel very soon and a lot of meetings were being held to decide what action we should take should this situation occur. As can well be imagined, our conversation consisted of nothing else.

At the beginning of September, the Italian guards in the sentry towers were behaving in a very odd fashion. They were shaking their own hands to signal to us that there had been an armistice; a great deal of coming and going was observed in the Italian barracks and all the ordinary Italian soldiers were wearing smiles a mile wide. They kept calling to us, '*la guerra é finita*' ('the war is over'). How little they knew!

The day wore on and we kept a close watch on all the activity in the Italian quarters Believe me, there was a great deal of it. As evening came, we all realised that there had been no evening roll call. Suddenly we got the order to get packed up, as we were moving out. The ensuing chaos beggared description.

The poor Italians were in a dreadful state, yelling. '*I tedeschi arriveranno presto*' and, in English, all at once 'the Germans are coming soon'. This helped to increase the panic to get packed and to get on the move.

I had no idea where Bob and Clicker, my two pals, were, but this was only secondary to getting out of the camp as quickly as possible. The Italians escorted us out of the back of the camp and marched us up the mountain behind the camp. They kept us on the move for about an hour or so, until we came to a ravine. Here we were told to bed ourselves down for the night, and they posted sentries all around us. It was noticed that they had a number of machine guns manned and that they were all pointing in our direction. We just didn't have a clue what they intended to do with us.

I don't believe anybody had much sleep that night. I know I didn't get a wink. I spent quite a time trying to find Bob and Clicker, but without success. When dawn broke we set about rustling up something from our Red Cross parcels for breakfast; we had to forgo brewing up because the fires would attract attention. As the morning wore on, we were still milling around in the ravine and I still hadn't set eyes on Bob or Clicker.

Eventually, at about midday, we were told to form up; we were about to move off to pastures new. This, however, was not to be. We were marched straight back into the camp. After the usual roll call, it was discovered that we were a number of prisoners short – some had seized the opportunity and made off into the blue. I was to find that Bob and Clicker were among the absentees.

A day or two later, all sorts of rumours were doing the rounds in the camp: we had landed in Genoa, Naples, Rome, Ancona and various other places. Then I got to thinking seriously of getting out of the place myself. The scheme that I came up with was to involve the daily routine with the 'gash box'. This was the name given to the rubbish box that I mentioned earlier. My idea was to post some lads up on the first floor, where, by looking out of the windows, there was a clear view of the pit where the rubbish was tipped; then to get into the box, cover myself with rubbish and just get tipped into the pit. The camp was right beside the main road, on the other side of which was a high hedge.

I had asked the lads at the window to give me the signal to climb out of the pit when the sentry in the corner tower was looking into the camp. I would then make a dash across the road and through the hedge. I did make a point of asking them to make sure that, when giving me the nod to move out of the pit, there was no traffic about. It worked like a charm. I was through the hedge like a rabbit and running as if I had an army after me, which, of course, I hadn't.

I've no idea what kept me running along that hedge for so

long; I'm sure I could have slowed down to a walk much sooner than I did. Perhaps it was just sheer exhilaration at having got out of the place. I found a hollow and rested up for a quarter of an hour or so, mainly to get my breath back, but also to take stock of the situation now that I was on the loose. My possessions consisted of the clothes that I stood up in and eighty Italian lire, not the camp money which was worthless outside – so I was not exactly in a very good situation. But it could have been worse: I could still be inside.

I decided to make a move and to get out of the valley and up into the mountains. A great deal of German traffic was on the road, all significantly going south. It was obvious that they were going to put up a lot of resistance down south. To get to the mountains it was necessary to re-cross the road, and to do this I had to wait quite some considerable time for a break in the traffic. Once across, I made for the high ground and just kept on climbing until I had an imposing view of the valley and the camp could be clearly seen.

It was late afternoon when I realised that I was beginning to feel rather hungry. I began to eat what was on offer; this was mainly nuts and grapes that were cultivated in odd patches of soil on the mountainside by the peasants. I was trying to avoid any sort of contact with anybody. All I wanted to do at this stage was stay out of sight and put as much distance as possible between me and the camp. The weather was definitely in my favour, very warm and dry, with a cloudless sky.

I had to do a lot of detouring to avoid civilians who were working on their smallholdings. Here and there they did spot me and, rather surprisingly to me, they gave me a wave, which I thought most unusual because I was still wearing my uniform. Perhaps they were thinking that I was German. I kept on until about 7 p.m. and then decided to look for some reasonably secure place to spend the night. I found a shepherd's shack that was just over the crest, completely out of sight of the road. I decided that this would be my lodging place for the night. It wasn't very clean – in fact it was quite a dirty little hut – so I set about clearing it of the rubbish that was inside.

Sleep was a long time coming and didn't last very long. I kept waking up and, each time I did, my mind was racing away with all sorts of thoughts. Eventually the dawn came and I realised that it was very cold indeed, so I set off walking straight away to get myself warmed up. I was to discover that all over these lower slopes of the Apennines there were tracks; these were made by the people of the region and their donkeys, when they were on their way to work on their patches of land. I was heading south and, at this moment, all I could see were mountains and more mountains.

After about an hour of this I was beginning to feel much warmer and hungrier. I soon came to the conclusion that, if I were to make my escape a success, I would have to think very seriously about organising food of some sort. To survive on nuts and grapes might be all right for a few days but this would be useless in the long term. As I kept on walking I could see in the distance a mountain village. I guessed this to be about two or three miles from where I was. I was to improve my judgement of distance in the mountains after this, because I reached the outskirts of this village about four hours later. It must have been about five miles distant at least, if not more.

I lay down and watched the village. I could see people meandering about and could clearly hear dogs barking. It appeared to be free of any traffic, as far as I could see. One house looked to be about eighty yards from the rest; it was separated from the village by a field with a crop of some sort in it and a big pen containing some hundred or so sheep. It had smoke coming from the chimney, so I presumed that it was occupied. I decided to approach this house and try out my Italian in the quest for some food. The front door was wide open so I gave a knock and said my prayers, because I had no idea how I would be received.

I was, in the event, to be very pleasantly surprised. A young woman answered my knock and, as soon as I let her know that I was after something to eat she called out for her father, who came to the door. Before I could say anything he looked at me and said, '*Buongiorno, inglesi*'. He realised that I was English even before I had spoken to him. He followed up with, '*Benvenuto, vieni dentro.*' He was telling me to come inside and that I was welcome. I was very surprised by this because I thought that they would have given me a more hostile reception. I don't think anybody had seen me approach the house so, as long as these two were in my sight, I shouldn't have too much to worry about.

I was given some hot soup that the girl warmed up for me and some bread and a glass of wine. I ate it up and expressed my gratitude to them for helping me, to which the old fellow replied: '*Niente, niente.*' In other words: 'It's nothing.' To me, it was quite something. Here was I; a few days ago I was their enemy, a soldier, yet here they were giving me food and helping me to make good my escape from the Germans. I had never expected to be received like this, so once again I thanked them and intimated that I would be moving on. It was then that I heard a phrase that I was to hear so often in the coming months. The old man said to me, '*Quando vengono gli inglesi?*' Translated this means, 'When are the English coming?'

So I replied that in a few days they would be here. Little did I know how far out that little forecast was going to be! The old chap rattled off something very fast in Italian and I understood not a word of it, as it was much too fast for me to follow. I then asked him his name and he told me it was Michele Troiani and that the girl, his daughter, was named Assuntina. It seems so strange to me that I only met these people for a little more than half an hour, yet I was never to forget their names.

The girl returned to the room with a little packet, done up in a piece of paper. She handed this to me with the words, '*Un po' piú di cibo per te*', which meant, 'a little more food for you.' I thanked them both and made ready to leave, at which the girl handed to me a little crucifix; they both warned me to '*stare molto attento*', which meant I was to be very alert. Before I left, I asked the old man if he had a map of the area and for the name of the village. He replied that the village was called Collebrincioni and he was sorry, but he didn't possess any maps. I thanked them both once again and made my departure, again heading away from the village and back up the mountains.

Once I had put a good distance between myself and the village I paused for a breather. Finding a well-shaded spot, I sat down and unwrapped the little parcel they had given me. It contained a piece of bread, some cheese, a small piece of sausage and an apple.

I sat and wondered what it could be that motivated these people to help me; after all, I was an enemy soldier, still in uniform. I thought that, were the roles reversed, I couldn't see this happening in England. Their attitude towards me changed my thinking about them. On escaping, I had thought that everybody I met would be an enemy, that I should trust nobody and that I must keep out of the sight and hearing of everybody or else I would end up back in the camp. This did not mean that I was going to accept that all the Italians would have the same attitude towards me, as this couple had. I was not that naïve.

I resumed my walk, heading, I hoped, in a southerly direction once again. I was using a track that was taking me towards a very large mountain. It was still many miles distant but it was so high that it dominated the landscape. I was to learn that this was the Gran Sasso – the highest mountain in the Apennines. It was while on this track that I first came into contact with some Italian soldiers who, because of the Armistice, had either been disbanded or had deserted – their sole object in life was to go home. As the days went by, these people were to become more numerous and there were many Italian officers among them, all with the same object – they simply wanted to go home. The civilians that worked their patches of land were very approachable and helpful; my impression was that they really believed that the war was over. They were entirely willing to give a little food to any of those travelling in the mountains; there was quite a large number of travellers.

After I had been out of the camp for about a week, I met an elderly Italian who had a mule with him. This man told me that his name was Archimedio Petrociani, and that he 'spika da inglesi', because many years ago he had lived in America. I humoured his English as much as I could, but I found that I could understand him much better when he spoke Italian! He was a very comical character and he gave me the news that all the prisoners in the camp at L'Aquila had been set free.

Very shortly this statement was to be proved correct because I began to meet a few of them up in the mountains. They told me that when the gates were opened at the camp the ensuing chaos had to be seen to be believed. These prisoners were roaming around in groups of all sizes. I met up with one group often, who had somehow got hold of some Italian rifles. I felt that, if escape was the primary motive for being out of the camp, then travelling in groups as large as this was simply asking for trouble and a swift return behind barbed wire. I carried on walking alone after this meeting with the riflemen because I was convinced that to travel in a large group was a very big mistake.

On that same day, about a couple of hours later, I could see in the distance another village. I decided to head for it and see if I could rustle up some more food. I had left the track and was walking higher up the mountain; it was now late afternoon and I could see, just below me, the villagers returning home after working their land. I decided to stop for a while to allow these people to reach their village, before I got too close to it.

After a short while, I spotted Archie the Italian American, this time without his mule. I tied to attract his attention because I felt he might be a good source of information on the village. He heard me calling his name and stopped and gave me a wave, so I clambered down to him. He told me that the village up ahead was indeed his village, that it was called Arischia, and that it wouldn't be a very good idea for me to go into it. The reason was that the village had a large regional carabinieri post, which was often visited by the Germans. The Italians called the Germans '*tedeschi*' and they were absolutely terrified of them. These poor people didn't have a great deal; Archie gave me to understand that if the Germans wanted anything, they just took it, with no question of payment. The Italian peasants really went in fear of them.

Archie told me that he knew of a good place where I could hide out, and that he would bring me something to eat the following day. So I fell in step with him along the track, until we came to a point where we left the track, descended about twenty metres and came to a crack in the rock face. This, said Archie, was it! Upon my squeezing through this crack, it opened out into a small chamber that was about nine feet deep and three feet wide, with headroom of about nine feet. As a hideout it was absolutely ideal; by standing just inside the entrance, I had a clear view of the village and of the main road that ran by the side of the settlement. This road reminded me of those that climbed the escarpments in the desert; it wound back and forth across the face of the mountain until it disappeared over the summit.

The following morning, as good as his word, Archie appeared with the promised food. He arrived very early; it must have been about 5 a.m. – long before any of the villagers left the village. For this I was very grateful, because the fewer people there were who knew where I was, the greater my security. He'd brought me some bread, cheese, nuts and a bottle of home-brewed vino; as an added surprise he gave me an old pair of trousers and a shirt. According to Archie, the Germans had carried out a '*rastrellamento*'; in English, this meant a round-up of many of the prisoners who had been released. He said that the camp was functioning once again but the guards were all Germans, He added that I should be very alert because there were many '*spie*' (spies) about because the Germans were offering a reward of 1,500 lire for every prisoner who was turned in. So now I had a price on my head.

I changed into the civvy shirt and trousers and gave Archie mine in return; I told him that I was hanging on to my battledress blouse because it was quite cold at night. He said that he wouldn't be able to come the next day but he was going to send his sister with '*qualche cosa*' ('something') and she would, like him, come very early. I thanked him for his help to which he replied, '*Niente! Niente!*' – in other words, he was saying that it was nothing. He made his way up to the track and went about his day's work, while I sat in my cave and had a little breakfast, washed down with his vino. A very potent brew it was too!

Sitting just inside the entrance to the cave, I had a clear view of the road and could see some German trucks winding their way along the mountainside. My mind was a mass of whirling thoughts. A few days ago I was stuck inside a prison camp with not much hope of getting home; now I was out of the camp but I was certainly no nearer home. In the camp I could, once a month, write to either my parents or my girlfriend; now they weren't going to get any news from me at all. I wondered whether, through the Red Cross, I would again be listed as missing.

I also realised that I could not stay holed up in this place for too long. Sometime or other, the locals would find out that I was here. Once this happened, I knew that I would be on my way back to the camp. Therefore, after about a week of living like a recluse, I made up my mind to get on the move once more. I said my farewell to Archie and thanked him again for all his help. I recall I told him that I would never forget what he had done for me. I never have!

By now September was drawing to a close and the evenings were beginning to become a little chilly. I realised that, if I was going to survive up in these mountains, I was going to have to organise myself a lot better. I needed a civvy jacket and a blanket of some sort for the cold nights to come. I left the cave behind me and set off once more, trusting that I was heading south. I thought to myself that at least I was certainly travelling light.

The next few days were a revelation to me because I met several other prisoners of various nationalities – Aussies, South Africans and British, all garbed in a variety of civilian clothing, all of whom were hopefully heading towards our troops down south. They had come from a number of different camps – Macerata, Chieti and Sulmona. Some of these chaps were quite sure of their objectives, others were much less so, but all of them had one hope in common and that was to stay one jump ahead of the Germans.

On the first night after leaving the cave I found a shepherd's hut to spend the night in; there were a lot of these scattered around the mountains. When I awoke the following morning and went to the door, I found that the hut was surrounded by sheep. A shepherd was sitting a short distance away with his dog, which set up a lot of barking on my appearance in the doorway. He calmed the dog down and beckoned me over to him. He told me he had looked into the hut, when he arrived there, saw that I was asleep, so had left me in peace to finish my slumbers. He said that his name was Maurizio and that he came from Arischia, the village that I had just left. He shared his lunch with me. This consisted of the usual dark brown bread and some garlic sausage, plus the good old bottle of home-brewed vino. Sitting talking to him, after we had eaten and I accepted a cigarette from him, my first for some little time, he told me that there were many Germans in Arischia and that down in the main valley in the city of L'Aquila were many more. I asked him how far away was the city and his reply rather took the wind out of my sails. He said it was about ten kilometres, which is a little over six miles. I was shattered by the news, as I had thought that I was much farther away. I told him that I had been to Collebrincioni and not too far off Arischia, and he drew on the ground with his stick and showed me that I had walked in a large semicircle. In other words I hadn't achieved much in putting any sort of distance between myself and the camp. He also confirmed that the Germans had recaptured a large number of my fellow prisoners and that the camp at L'Aquila was pretty full.

He let me know that his brother was coming up later that same day to relieve him for two days and that, if I stayed there until he returned, he would bring me an old jacket and a blanket. I thanked him very much and told him that I would be only to glad to hang on for a couple of days if I were to get a blanket at the end of it. So it turned out that a couple of days later I had a civvy jacket and a blanket; he also brought a large piece of bread and some cheese and a bottle of vino, plus some leaves of tobacco and cigarette papers. He also gave me a small pocket knife. The generosity of these people towards me was astounding!

Chapter Eight

I was beginning to find that I had an aptitude for picking up the Italian language quickly. No doubt my grammar was appalling, but it was, at that stage anyway, only necessary to make myself understood. In this I was having a great deal of success. I wondered how the war was going. Conversations with the Italians on this topic were very confusing indeed: one would say the Allies had reached one town and the next one you spoke to would say that they were nowhere near it. All very disheartening! How I would have loved to get hold of a radio and tune in to the news from London. This was not to happen for quite some time, but it did eventually.

A couple of days after saying farewell to Maurizio and his sheep, I could see below me a mountain stream. As I had not had a bath for so long, I decided to go down to it to see if I could clean myself up a little bit. It was still quite warm during the day and the sun was shining brilliantly. I thought I would dry myself with my blanket and then lay it out to dry in the sun.

I followed the stream down until it skirted some stunted acacias and decided that this was sufficiently secluded for me to take a bath. I stripped off and stepped into the water. It surprised me how cold it was; it really took my breath away. I rubbed myself as best I could because I had no soap. I thought to myself, I might not be really clean but I am certainly very refreshed. It was as I was drying myself on my blanket that I nearly jumped out of my skin. A voice said, from behind me, 'I bet you enjoyed that.' I whirled around and saw Jim Kerr, one of my friends from the camp at L'Aquila. He had almost given me heart failure and I told him so.

Once I had got dressed, we sat and began swapping experiences. It appeared that Jim had been among those who had been set free en bloc from the camp. His tale was very similar to my own except that he had at first gone across to the other side of the valley, towards a village called Coppito. He found that there were many Germans stationed in the village and they were, in fact, the outfit who were responsible for the round-up of prisoners earlier on. So he had cut back across the valley to put, as he said, a lot of space between himself and the Germans. We were delighted to have found each other and after a long conversation we decided to team up and see if we could make it to our lines together.

A few days later we were walking along a track and the view we had of the valley down below was magnificent. Suddenly we could see up ahead a man walking towards us; he was accompanied by a large dog. As we approached each other, Jim and I decided that, as he had obviously seen us, there was no point to turning tail and running and we would have to play it by ear. On getting closer, Jim said to me, 'I know this chap – I worked with him on the building site in L'Aquila.'

Jim's job was to assist the chief engineer on the site, and here that man was, walking toward us. When we met, this fellow was all over us – handshakes all round and much backslapping. It appeared he had been to see some relations in one of the villages and was now on his way home – and would we please be his guests in his home, where we could get a proper bath and a change of clothing? This was too good an offer to turn down so we changed direction and accompanied him along the track until it started to descend towards the main road. We then asked him where exactly his home was, and his reply startled us somewhat. It was standing all by itself surrounded by fields right alongside the main road. We told him that we felt it would be too much of a risk for us to take. He brushed our protests aside and assured us that there was no danger, so we decided that the promise of a change of clothes, a bath and some food was just too big a carrot to turn down.

On arrival at his house, he introduced us to his wife, who, with much wringing of her hands and the words '*poverini, poverini*' (which meant 'poor things, poor things'), set about making us welcome. This house was totally different from those of the villagers, being modern, spacious and generally well appointed. The first thing she organised for us was a bath. The sheer luxury of it was an absolute boost to our morale. We were then each given clean vest, pants, shirt and trousers. We felt really human once again.

This chap told us that up to a couple of days ago he had some Germans billeted on him. They had an ack-ack gun in the field alongside. This information made us a little uneasy and Jim and I exchanged glances, which was noticed by our host, who said: '*non abbiate paura perché i tedeschi andranno via*' – in other words, we were not to be frightened because the Germans had gone away.

His wife, meanwhile, had been busy preparing the evening meal. What a spread it was! Jim remarked that not only did the villagers have poorer houses, but the same applied to the quality of the food. We had started the meal with a large plate of pastasciutta, followed by chicken and salad, with the bottle of wine going the rounds; this was followed by cheese and fruit and it was all rounded off with the coffee pot An absolutely marvellous meal and our thanks were very profuse indeed.

After the meal we sat and talked for an hour or so and then the lady of the house suggested that it was time for us to go to bed. They had insisted that we stay the night and we could resume our wanderings in the morning. We were shown into a bedroom upstairs that contained a large double bed, and after exchanging *buona notte*s, we were left to ourselves. Jim and I sat on the bed talking for a while. We couldn't believe our luck in bumping into his boss like this and to have been given a meal, the like of which we hadn't had in ages! Eventually we turned in and were soon fast asleep.

We were suddenly shaken out of our slumbers by our host, with his fingers to his lips, signalling to us that we were to be silent. We could hear voices outside the house calling '*Raus, raus!*' This we knew was German and it meant, 'Come on, get moving.' Our host had whipped all the clothing off our bed and was putting it on the floor in his own bedroom, where his wife was sitting up in bed with her fingers to her lips. He indicated to us that we were to bed down on the floor at the foot of his bed and then went out of the bedroom and locked the door.

He went downstairs and we could hear voices down below. After about an hour he returned to us again, with his finger to his lips. He locked the door from the inside and crouched down beside us and whispered to us that the Germans were spending the night in the bed we had just vacated. We were to be very quiet! They would be leaving in the morning. This was absolutely incredible. Here were we, escaped prisoners of war, on the run in Italy, and we were sleeping in the next room to a couple of the enemy.

Needless to say, Jim and I spent a sleepless night. The next morning the husband and wife got up early, dressed themselves then left the bedroom; before leaving they gave us the sign for '*silencio*', a finger to their lips, and on leaving once again they locked the door. We could hear voices downstairs and we presumed that they were giving the Germans some breakfast. We were locked in the bedroom for around two hours before we heard their wagon being started up, and eventually roaring off.

Immediately the husband came up and unlocked the door, asking us if we were all right. He was very calm and collected. I really did admire this man. We went downstairs to be greeted with a good morning from his wife, who asked us if we had been frightened. I didn't know the Italian for petrified so I just answered in the negative, Oh no, we weren't frightened at all. Not much! The husband told us that the Germans were a couple of those who had been with the ack-ack guns in the field outside his house. They had been sent back to retrieve something or other that had been left behind and that we were not to worry. He was a very cool customer indeed.

After we had eaten our breakfast we took our leave of this extremely brave couple and retraced our steps back up to the same track we had left when we had met up with Jim's old boss. We were now having frequent encounters with Italians who were in the mountains, those who were there to work and those who, like us, were on the run from the Germans. They gave us all sorts of advice and news of Allied advances, all of which were at best wildly inaccurate and in most cases totally false. They were living almost completely on word of mouth and, as the word was passed on from one to the other, it got embroidered a wee bit more.

We then we crossed the main road once again. We skirted round a village named San Vittorino. We saw Germans and their vehicles in this village. It seemed to me that the Germans were more likely to be in the villages near the main roads, rather than those that were more inaccessible. Jim agreed with me, so we decided that, as far as it was possible, we would avoid any village that was anywhere near the main roads. Late in the afternoon we met an old Italian who told us that his name was Pasquale; he had been working on a plot of land that he owned and was on his way home. He asked us where we would be sleeping and I replied, '*Per terra*' – on the ground. He said that this was not good and he knew a place where we could get some shelter.

He walked with us for about half an hour until we came to his plot of land; this, by Italian standards was quite a large plot. It was situated in a broad gully lying in dead ground from the valley. We couldn't be seen from the valley unless we were to walk up to the crest. It appeared to be an ideal spot for us to hole up for a while. At the back of his plot was the shelter that he had told us about. This was a man-made hole in the ground, with a very narrow, well-concealed entrance, with stunted bushes growing right across it. The roof was made of logs that had been laid across the hole and covered with about three feet of soil. This must have been done a long time ago, because this soil had a healthy growth of grass and weeds; it looked just like a natural mound. Pasquale took us down the end of the gully and round the contour of the mountain side. To the left he showed us a mountain stream. He gave us to understand that the water was good to drink, and indeed it was crystal clear and icy cold. It tasted wonderful. So we had been set up in a reasonably safe lodging place with fresh water to hand and some food that our benefactor of the previous evening had given us on our departure. We thought that we weren't doing too badly. We had no way of knowing how it would all turn out in the end, but we were both beginning to feel just a little more hopeful.

The following morning, Pasquale arrived and greeted us with much warmth, asking us how we had slept. He gave us some food that had been prepared for us by his wife. We were to learn that her name was Bettina. He then went on to tell the astonishing news they were hiding '*uno Scozzese, si chiama Carlo*' – a Scotsman, named Charles – in their house. I asked him the name of his village and he told me that it was called Cansatessa Pettino and that it was about three kilometres away. We couldn't see it from the crest, because, as the mountain contour went round to the left, it put the village just out of our sight. The food that Pasquale had brought out with him was our first taste of a delicacy called *chi chi*. This was a large kind of pea, cooked in some kind of sauce – very tasty indeed but, more importantly, very filling.

We stayed in this place for a couple of weeks, reasonably secure, with Pasquale bringing us something to eat pretty regularly. But Jim and I both felt that, seeing that the fighting down south seemed to be at a bit of a stalemate, we should start thinking of trying to get further south. It was, by now, getting to the end of October and the weather was beginning to break up. We were having a lot of rain and our cave, being below ground level, was at times more than a little unpleasant.

Therefore, one day while sitting talking to Pasquale, we told him of our intention to resume our trek down south. He did everything he could to dissuade us, pointing out to us that the front line was pretty static and therefore would be almost impossible to get through. He then asked us if we had any idea what the weather was like in the mountains during the winter months, to which we had to reply that we had no idea. He then gave us a graphic description that really gave us something to think about. He told us that the next four months – that was through to the end of February – were not the months to attempt any long-term walking. After he had left us once again to our own devices, we sat and talked it over, but now we were more subdued in our desire to set off once again. We had to agree that there was a great deal to be said for what Pasquale had told us.

We finally made up our minds to try to hang on and see the winter out before moving, but we both agreed that it would be prudent to have somewhere else to sleep, because, by now, we were becoming known to people from several villages around, and we assumed that at least some of them would know exactly where we were sleeping.

I had already told Jim about my 'crack in the mountain' that looked out over the village of Arischia, so we made up our minds to go and see if it had new tenants. Before leaving, we told

Pasquale our intention and he told us to try to contact the family called Ragone, who, he told us, would help us. He wished us good luck and when we actually parted he was crying. What can one write that can actually describe the goodness, the kindheartedness, of these people? It's just beyond me! It was obvious that these people had very little in the way of worldly goods, yet they were so willing to help others such as us who, I suppose, were even worse off.

While we were trekking across to Arischia, we once again met up with our shepherd, Maurizio. He told me to be very careful, because there were many Germans in 'Campo Santo'. Jim asked me what he had said, so I replied that we had to avoid a village called Campo Santo, because of the presence of a lot of Germans. This caused quite a laugh later on as my Italian got better and I discovered that *campo santo* was the name that they gave to a cemetery. We found out later that this cemetery, just outside the village of Arischia, had a long drive up to the entrance gates and the Germans were using the drive as an ammo dump.

Maurizio had his sister with him; she was named Leontina and was dressed in the usual female peasant's garb of all black. It appeared to us that they were in permanent mourning for some member of the family. She had brought him up some supplies of food and drink to sustain him for his stay in the mountains. It was a fact of life for these shepherds to spend more time seeking pasture for their sheep than they spent at home. We were given something to eat and drink, and also some bread and cheese to take with us. Before we set off once again, Maurizio warned us to be careful and not to put too much trust in everybody we met, because there were still many Fascists about, who were looking for escaped prisoners for the reward money.

We found my previous home a couple of hours later; it was not occupied, so we settled in. Just a couple of days later we had a visit from Archimedio, who told us to our astonishment that Leontina had seen him and told him that we were heading for Arischia and that Pasquale had got a message to the Ragone family about us. The bush telegraph between these villages was extremely effective. It made us realise that we were becoming well known in this particular area and we hoped that those who did know of our whereabouts would keep it to themselves.

Then began a steady stream of visitors to our hiding place, all bringing us some little comfort or other, plus dire warnings to keep ourselves well out of sight of others. It was a very strange experience; Jim and I used to sit and talk about it and came to the conclusion that they had sort of adopted us. We realised, of course, that this couldn't go on for too much longer because there were, by now, too many people who knew of our cave and it only needed one word in the wrong ear and we would be for the high jump. There was no way that we wanted a return to captivity, so we began planning our next move. We decided that, when we took off, we would tell nobody, so that the word wouldn't spread that we were about to depart. Although to leave without thanking everybody we knew for their help seemed to be a pretty nasty act, we reckoned it to be the safest way to go about it.

We decided to move the following morning, but before we went we were to be given a terrific morale boost late in the afternoon. We were sitting on the side of our mountain watching a convoy of German trucks climbing the road that wound its way above Arischia when suddenly they were being attacked by British aircraft. The planes were lining up in the sky to swoop down and strike the column of trucks with machine gun and cannon fire. They scored many hits. There was plenty of smoke and flames coming from the trucks and there we were – the two of us standing up, cheering our heads off. We felt really great; it made us feel that we were just that bit closer to our own people, just by being able to see them whipping about in the sky.

We were off at first light the next day, before any of the locals had begun to make their way to their plots. It felt good to be on the move once more and we set off at a good pace. The weather was holding up; it was dry, but a bit chilly. This was to be expected, because by now it was mid-November. When we paused at about midday for a bite of bread and cheese, we realised that we had been out of sight of the main road all morning and, on the route we had chosen, which was a bit lower than the one I had first taken to Arischia, we hadn't met a soul. This struck us as strange because wandering about up in these mountains had got us used to seeing people, even if they were only in the distance, but today we had seen nobody. Trudging on after our meal, we realised that the track we were on was steadily taking us down lower and after a while the road once again came into view. Walking towards us with a donkey was an old man. The donkey was laden on both sides with bundles of wood, which had probably been gathered for firewood. He pulled the donkey to a halt and we met and he said: '*Buongiorno, voi siete inglesi.*' This meant: 'Good day, you are English.' Here we were, dressed in old civvy rags, nothing at all about us to suggest this to the military, yet this little old guy had even got our nationality correct.

He was from the village of Cansatessa Pettino and he wanted to show us a place where we could stay the night. '*Molto sicuro,*' he said. This meant 'very safe'. But we felt that we wanted to get a bit further on, so we thanked him and said that we had to be moving much farther from the road, before we felt safe. He wished us '*Buona fortuna*' (or 'Good luck'), gave us a wave and was on his way. We were to come across this great little character at a later date; he was to be a really good friend to both of us, yet at that stage we didn't even know his name.

We kept on going until the light began to fail and then we started to keep our eyes peeled for somewhere to hole up for the night. In fact, we were too low down the mountain for there to be any shepherds' huts and, not finding any cave that we could get into, we had to settle for a night in the open. We found a small hollow that hid us from the road and prepared to get our heads down. Fortunately for us it was a dry night and we were able to sleep reasonably well. We had many nights like this one, sleeping in the open, and we always woke up chilled right through, very willing to move on to get some warmth back into our bodies.

One day we met an old civilian who told us that there were some more POWs about three kilometres from where we were and that they were all living in the village of San Vittorino. He told us that these men had been in the village for several weeks – we did not like the sound of this at all. So we asked directions and thanked him. We then set off once more, deciding to avoid that particular place, as it seemed to us to be over-populated.

A couple of hours after we had said our farewell to the old man from San Vittorino, we encountered another elderly gent, who gave us to understand that he would guide us to a really safe and secure place to stay. We fell in step with this old boy and he began to take us once again upwards towards a copse of trees. Once we arrived there, we had an absolutely superb view of the valley down below. He took us through the trees and beyond, until we came to a crevice in the side of the mountain, very similar to the one we stayed in at Arischia. It was a first-class hideout. We could see anything approaching us for miles in all directions. We were happy to make this place our home for a while. He told us that he would be sending us up something to eat as soon as he returned to his village and asked us not to light any fires – '*per via del fumo*' – because the smoke would be seen for miles.

He was as good as his word, because about an hour or so later we could see him returning, accompanied by a woman with a basket balanced on her head. When they reached us we were greeted by '*buona sera*' – 'good evening' – from both of them and the man then told us that the lady was his '*moglia*' (wife). They sat down beside us and started to uncover the basket. What a feast was set out in front of us! There was bread, cheese, nuts, grapes, tomatoes and fresh figs, plus a bottle of wine. We were very profuse in our thanks to them, to which the man simply replied, '*Niente, niente!*' It might have been very little to him, but to us it was unbelievable generosity. We were very grateful to them and just couldn't thank them enough. The man's name was Amerigo Marchetti and his wife was called Ausilia and they came from the village of Cansatessa Pettino, which was the village right alongside the main road.

After they had departed, Jim and I sat talking and tried to find some explanation for the attitude that these people had towards us. We both agreed that if the roles were reversed it would be an entirely different situation. We finally came to the conclusion that these people would help just about anybody who was in need without any thought about the retribution that was liable to fall upon them should they be discovered. It was a sobering thought.

Ausilia was to wend her way up to us every evening just about dusk for a number of weeks to come. She would sit beside us and watch us set about the food she had brought up to us, all the time saying, as if to herself, '*poveri figli di mamma*,' – this meant: 'poor children of mothers'. She said this constantly, almost as if she were talking to herself, and it was to be some time before I was to really understand the reason for her constant use of this phrase.

We were ambling along one day to fill our water bottles at a mountain stream, only about 500 yards from our hideout, when we spotted a couple heading in our direction. There was no point in beating a retreat, because we knew that they had seen us. We reached the water before them and proceeded to fill our bottles. As they drew nearer we could see that they were not peasants by any means. They were holding hands and, at a guess, I would have said that they were in their late twenties; both were very well dressed. The man had a small rucksack on his back and as they came up to us he said, 'Good morning, how are you both?' in perfect English. I asked him in Italian why he thought we were English. He laughed and said, 'We came out to find you so that we could all have a cup of tea together. I have everything that we need in my rucksack.' He introduced himself as Giulio Morelli, and his companion was his wife, Alfonsina. He told us that he had set out to find Alfredo and 'Jeemy', and he was very pleased to have succeeded. We shook hands all round and he at once set about getting the tea on the go. He had, as he said, all the gear needed in his rucksack. This couple, and indeed Giulio's family were to become very good friends to us in the weeks and months to come.

After we had our tea, we sat chatting on the mountainside and we discovered that Giulio was a very interesting character indeed. It appeared that he used to work in Rome in the Cinecittà – this meant the 'film city'. He used to be a film director, but he had made a film that was critical of Mussolini and his Fascisti and for that he had been banned from making films. He had therefore come out to live in his family's country house, which was just outside the village of Pettino. His father was known in Pettino as 'Il Capitano' and we were to learn later that he was indeed a retired army captain who had fought on our side in World War I. It was a very interesting couple of hours that we spent talking to them. When they left us they said that they would be up to visit us again very soon.

When they had gone, Jim and I were trying to evaluate this couple; we asked ourselves whether they were sincere or whether they had been sent up to find out how many prisoners were still on the loose in the area. They had appeared to be totally convincing to us, but on the other hand we desperately wanted to remain free and eventually to meet up with our own people. So we decided to move our location once more – not to leave the area, just our hideout. We had no desire whatsoever to go back behind barbed wire; it was therefore only common sense to take the precaution of a move. We finished up in another shepherd's hut, much higher up the mountain.

Each evening we would descend the mountain to our meeting place with Ausilia and the food that she was bringing out to us. Jim and I both agreed that we should suggest to her that we were both very fit and that either of us could come very much lower down the mountain to meet her, as this at least would make her self-imposed task to feed us a little bit easier. This she agreed to and she pointed out a house to us that stood all on its own on a track that was known as Via Arischia Vecchio. This was a track that ran from the village of Arischia all the way to the city of L'Aquila. We were to watch hundreds of villagers trudging along that track with their donkeys, taking something or other into the city to sell. Ausilia told us she would meet us just at the back of this house, which was owned by some very good friends of her and her family. This was the house of a couple named Innamorati; the man was called Pasquale and his wife's name was Bettina. These two were a wonderful couple whom we had met earlier; to me they appeared to have no fears of the Germans whatsoever. They were a truly remarkable pair. They had a Scotsman named Charlie Harvey whom they were hiding in their home and I would point out that their house was right alongside the track known as the Via Arischia Vecchio and that there were scores and scores of people passing the front door each and every day. This couple asked Jim and I to have our evening meal, which Ausilia was bringing out to us, in her house instead of sitting on the mountainside. This we declined because we felt that they were taking a big enough risk with having Charlie in their home all the time. Furthermore we did not relish the risk to our own little bit of freedom that we were enjoying for the first time for two and a half years.

We were to continue this routine of climbing up and down the mountain for another couple of weeks and we were both feeling pretty fit because of the exercise. We were still seeing the odd POW trekking across the mountains, and some of them were very odd indeed. We met and chatted to all sorts of people, who all had their own ideas and goals. Some were heading for the coast to pinch a boat, some were going to get within a few miles of the front and then lie up, waiting for the day that our lads would attack and let the front roll past them. One officer we met was heading for a certain monastery that he knew which was just outside Foggia. He intended to hide there until the front swept past; we wished him good luck. Many and varied were the intentions of these people but they all had one thing in common – not one of them wanted any more barbed wire.

One evening, it was arranged with Ausilia that we would, on the following evening, accompany her into the village to visit a house, the owner of which was a barber. It was almost three months since we had had our hair cut so we were very pleased with the offer, although we did have certain reservations about going into the village. It was a bit like going into the unknown, but we both felt that it was a chance we had to take, because our hair was making us look a bit like tramps. So the following evening found us walking along the Via Arischia Vecchio towards the village with our guardian angel Ausilia. I must admit that I was more than a little apprehensive about going into the place, because of its close proximity to the main road.

It was quite dark when we reached the village and, as we entered the place, I think that just about every dog in the locale started to bark. I remember thinking that we were doing our best to be as silent as we possibly could and here were the dogs letting everybody know that there was somebody in the vicinity. When we finally arrived at Ausilia's house, there was another woman waiting outside. We were told that this lady would be taking Jim to her home to eat; we were not to be afraid because she was entirely trustworthy and her husband was strongly anti-Fascist. So off went Jim with his benefactor and I entered the home of Ausilia for the first time.

It was a very poor place; it had a stone-flagged floor and a large open fireplace with a chain hanging from under the mantel. On the end of the chain was a huge pot dangling above a fire of twigs and bits of tree branches. It had a very smoky atmosphere. It became obvious to me that these people were extremely poor, with very few possessions, scarcely the most elementary things. For instance, there was a table and three chairs that were as old and decrepit as the sort of stuff that back home a junk shop would throw out.

I asked Ausilia when we would be going to the barber. She replied that first we would eat, and then we were to meet Jim at the barber's at 9 p.m., so it would seem that they had made arrangements for us to really get a haircut. While she busied herself with preparing the meal, I can recall thinking that much of what was happening to me would not be believed back home. After a short while, her husband Amerigo came home from work. He was employed in the city of L'Aquila and he was a miller. His employer, he said, was very rich; he owned a lot of land around this particular village and Amerigo used to work on much of it in the evenings and weekends. At harvest time his boss would come down and take about ninety per cent of the crop and the remaining ten per cent was Amerigo's payment for working the land. What a feudal arrangement!

While Ausilia went about her business, preparing the evening meal, Amerigo tried to hold a conversation with me. He had no English at all and I had a very difficult time trying to understand what he was saying. The reason for this was very laughingly explained to me by Ausilia. '*Lui parla sempre in dialetto*,' she said. This meant that he always spoke in the local dialect and it was to be some time before I was to be able to pick up sufficient of it to be able to hold a reasonable conversation with him. I was able to discover that his eldest son, named Alarico, was in the army in Africa and that they received no news of him for some months.

After we had eaten, I was taken by Ausilia to the barber's house, which was not in Cansatessa but farther up the track towards a place named Pettino. We were greeted very warmly by this barber and his family. Jim was already there and he was having his locks shorn. I was given a glass of wine by the man's wife and she immediately gave me a torrent of Italian, of which I could glean only the odd word here and there. I had to use an Italian phrase, one that I was to use many times in the future: 'Please would you speak slowly? I will then be able to understand you.' These people were very forthcoming; they were fed up to the back teeth with the war and they were heavily critical of Mussolini. Now, whether this was because the tide had turned or if they had felt that way since the start of the war, I couldn't know, and felt it was prudent not to ask them. When the barber had cut my hair, both Jim and I thanked him very much indeed and said our farewells to him and his family. We had no way of knowing that we would visit this house again in the future.

We walked back down the track to Cansatessa. We didn't meet a soul on the way. We thanked Ausilia for the meal and the haircut, wished her good night and made our way back to our hideout. I remember the night of the haircut very well because Jim and I lay and talked for a long time. We were amazed at the lengths these people were prepared to go to help us, while we realised there were probably just as many Italians who would turn us in at the drop of a hat We appreciated also that many of the people that we had met did appear to have an awful lot of respect for us when we told them that we were British. I think this was because they had a distorted view of our people; they didn't really believe that poverty existed in Britain. To them we were members of the British Empire, of the richest country in the world, and therefore were all of us well-off people. They were well off target, but we could never convince any of them otherwise. Jim reckoned that we shouldn't even try to persuade them, because what they thought about us wouldn't make much difference to our position anyway. In other words, let them think what they will, because to us *non fa niente* – it didn't matter.

Chapter Nine

We had now been out of the camp for a little more than a couple of months and were beginning to feel just a touch more confident of our chances of making our new-found freedom permanent. It was not a case of doing anything that was at all foolhardy. In no way did we feel secure and safe; at no time did we let our guard down. Perhaps it was just the fact that we had avoided being recaptured and felt that with lots of luck we could we could continue to do so.

One Sunday morning, we had another visit from Giulio and Alfonsina Morelli. They had arrived quite early and soon had the water boiling for the tea that they had once again kindly brought along with them. This couple were very good indeed to Jim and me. Giulio had brought along two shirts and two sweaters that were gratefully received. It was a kind thought on his part. They had come up to see us, mainly to invite us to the home of Captain Morelli, Giulio's father, to have a meal with them one evening. It was arranged that we should go down to their house on the Wednesday at 7 p.m.

This was to become quite an adventure because about to crop up were some difficulties that nobody could have foreseen. We tried to make ourselves as smart as we could for our trip down the mountain to the Morelli household. Their home was very substantial and it was obvious that they were rather well-off people. At the approach to their house was a drive of about seventy-five yards, with large trees on either side of the road; at the start of this drive was an enormous pair of metal gates.

So it was that at about 6.50 on the appointed evening that Jim and I turned into the gates, before executing a smart about-turn and retracing our steps. The drive was full of German vehicles that were pulled off the drive and dispersed among the trees and, of course, there were a good number of German soldiers milling about. We tried to appear as casual as possible while walking back towards the village, but I can vividly recollect to this day the way I felt inwardly – absolute turmoil! It had certainly given us the frighteners. We expected any second a German voice to be yelling at us to '*Alt hands hoch!*' but it didn't come. Lady Luck was sitting on our shoulders.

We remembered that the hairdresser in the village had a telephone and we decided to call in, to see if we could ring the Morellis to explain to them our reason for not being available for dinner. I made the call and, talking to Giulio, was really astonished when he said that we should retrace our steps and make the visit. He explained that the Germans had told them that they were only harbouring there for the night and would be away at first light. He said we should just walk down the drive and to give the Germans a greeting of '*Buona sera*', only if spoken to.

I told him we would do this and put the phone down. Jim then asked what he had said, so I told him. Jim's reply was that I must be joking, but I pointed out to him that we were dressed in civilian clothes and that the Jerries would not be expecting two escaped British prisoners to be calmly strolling past them. Furthermore, if we did not go, wouldn't the Morellis think we were windy? To which Jim replied that they could think what the hell they liked because he thought the whole thing was too risky.

We were having a glass of wine with the hairdresser when Jim suddenly said that he had thought it over and he was now in agreement with me. We should go because, as he saw it, he couldn't have any Italian thinking that we didn't have the guts to make the visit. So we thanked the barber and his wife for the phone call and the wine and once again set out for the Morellis' house. This time, knowing what was there waiting for us, we turned into the gates and started to walk up the drive, as if we had done it every day of our lives. Several Germans looked at us, but showed no interest in us at all. Only one spoke to us and he simply said '*Buona sera*' to which I replied in kind. Then we were at the door and were quickly welcomed inside by Giulio, who had a huge grin on his face. Introductions followed and we met Giulio's father and brother Lorenzo, and of course Alfonsina. There was, I remember, a lot of banter about our exploits in visiting them with the Germans just outside the door. They gave us an excellent meal, washed down with plenty of very old wine. I remember the Captain proudly showing us his World War I medals, among which was the British Military Cross, of which he was very proud indeed. He won this award fighting the Austrians, in the north of Italy.

We had a nice sing-song in English around the piano and it was an evening that is etched indelibly in my mind – one I will never forget as long as I live. Even as this was going on, I was asking myself why these people were doing this; why were they taking such risks to help us like this? There couldn't be any reward in it for them. Perhaps in some way it gave them a kind of satisfaction.

That evening in Giulio's home we felt more civilised than we had been for some considerable time, despite the fact that parked just outside the house was a large number of the enemy. During the evening, Giulio busied himself with taking some snaps of us and, although I was not to see the results of his skill with the camera while I was in Italy, I did nevertheless become the recipient of one of these snaps some forty-four years later.

At about 10.30 p.m. we said our goodbyes to the Morellis, after thanking them most profusely for the meal, their company and for their very great kindness. Jim and I, once again, began our walk down the Morellis' long drive amid all the German trucks. This time nobody at all spoke to us and I must confess that, when we reached the track that led back to the village, I let out a great sigh of relief. We had got away with it. Afterwards I was to think that, on the whole, it was a pretty foolhardy escapade and, if we valued our freedom, it would be wise to be a lot more careful in the future.

We decided not to walk through the village on our return trip, because we knew that we would only set all the dogs off howling, so after a hundred yards or so we swung off to our right and set off straight up the mountain to return to our hideout. We had to stop for a breather on a number of occasions, probably because we had eaten rather well. It must have been around 2 a.m. before we finally arrived back and settled down for some sleep. We lay there talking about the evening we had just spent for some little while before we finally nodded off.

Once again, our presence was beginning to become known to a large number of people and we again decided that, very shortly, we would have to be on the move to a new place somewhere. This was decided for us very soon, because one evening, when we came down the mountain for our evening meal, brought to us, as usual, by Ausilia, she was accompanied by her youngest son, Angelo. When we told him of our decision to find another place, he told us that he would come up to us the following day and he would show us a place that was '*molto sicuro*' – very safe. He was as good as his word. Nice and early the next morning he arrived, bringing a few cigarettes that he had scrounged from some Jerries for us. He told us that there were other English prisoners on the mountain who were being cared for by some of the people in his village, and that the place he was taking us to was much nearer to the village. It would be easier for his mother to bring us our evening meal. So we packed our few belongings and set off in file behind Angelo. This time we were heading down the mountain, so the going was a great deal easier. We finally fetched up down in the valley and were wondering just how much farther we were going because we were very near to the main road, a matter of about one hundred yards or so.

Angelo took us into a thick copse of trees and eventually came to a halt. He said to us with a big smile on his face, 'Well, this is it. This is very secure – no one will ever find you here!'

We looked around us and asked him where we should sleep. He replied that he would show us exactly where we would sleep, and he did. We were actually standing about three yards from it and we hadn't even seen it. It was a superb hideout, completely concealed by bushes right across its entrance. It was a hole in the ground with three steps going down, cut out of the earth. It opened up into a chamber that was approximately six feet deep by eight feet wide and five feet high, so its only drawback was that it wasn't possible to stand upright. Jim said that, although it was down in the valley, it had one great advantage: there were no tracks going back and forth, so there was less chance of all the people from different villages getting to know of our whereabouts. I could only agree with him as far as that was concerned. The village of Cansatessa, in which Angelo lived, was only about a quarter of a mile distant, so it would be that much easier for his mother Ausilia to bring us our meal every evening.

Angelo took us to the edge of the trees and pointed out to us the track to Arischia and also the home of Pasquale and Bettina, the couple who had Charlie Harvey living with them in their house. We were very pleased indeed with our new place of concealment and thanked Angelo for his help, to which he replied with the usual Italian response: 'Niente, niente'.

We settled in to our new abode and Jim and I decided that when leaving the place we would always walk to the rear of the cave, because this was really well covered by the trees; we could then set off for wherever we wished without highlighting the entrance.

During the next few weeks, we were to make the acquaintance of some of the other lads that Angelo had told us about, who were in the village and surrounding areas. The first one we knew was, of course, Charlie Harvey, who was living in the home of Bettina and Pasquale. Then there were Sid (Cyril) Courtney and Leslie Law, both of the Rifle Brigade. Jim knew both of these chaps from his unit in the desert. There was a fellow from the Navy named Norman Hartley and another prisoner, whom we called the Duke. This one lived with a family just outside the village. We didn't see a great deal of him; he appeared to spend most of his time inside the house and rarely ventured out, but when we did see him he was always well dressed – hence our dubbing him the Duke. There was another Londoner named Tommy Yoxall, who was, if I remember correctly, a member of the Green Howards. Incidentally, I was not to know the name of the Duke until some forty years later and in the most amazing circumstances. Each of these people I have mentioned was being looked after by a family in the village, and it is therefore not surprising that the name of this village is indelibly inscribed in my mind.

There was a family in the village named Innamorati who had two sons, both of whom were in the carabinieri. They were named Torquarto and Gino. These two were to be very helpful indeed to us. If they got word, for instance, that there was to be a '*rastrellamento*' – in other words, a round-up or raid by the Germans or Fascists – we would be tipped off in ample time to make ourselves very scarce indeed. These two people were staunch allies to us and I am convinced that they saved our bacon on at least two occasions.

Angelo and his mother continued to bring out our evening meal and we got into the habit of meeting them halfway. They always brought us the current news, but we nearly always found out afterwards that their reports were invariably wishful thinking. The rumours transmitted from village to village, embroidered in the telling and retelling, were sometimes almost beyond belief. We had landed at just about anywhere there was to land in Italy, parachutists had been dropped here there and everywhere – in days they would be here to liberate us. All of which, of course, was optimistic fantasy, because by now it was nearly Christmas and the fighting had become bogged down, mainly due to the weather, which was really beginning to bite. We had had a few light falls of snow, the temperature had fallen to near zero and we were really feeling it when we settled down for the night in our hole in the ground.

Christmas came and went. I honestly can't remember much about that particular period; I vividly recall the New Year, though. We were still residing in our hole just one hundred yards or so from the main road and, when the evening meal arrived, they had brought along a gift of a bottle of vino for the New Year. After they had departed, we had a visit from Pasquale with a gift for the New Year: another bottle of vino. By now Sid Courtney had joined Jim and I in our hideout and all three of us proceeded to get very happy indeed on the contents of the two bottles. We did not venture outside our hole, though, except when nature called, because we all three knew that we were very much inebriated, but we still retained sufficient caution to take no chances with our freedom.

We awoke on New Year's Day with throbbing heads and I remember Sid saying that he was going to pop into the city (L'Aquila) to purchase some aspirins. What a hope! When they came out with the evening meal they did have some news for us, however. They had decided that we could no longer carry on living in our hole in the ground, because the weather was now much too hard. They wanted us to move into the village.

Everything had been arranged for us, but of course we couldn't all be together. We would each be going to a separate house and we would have to spend most of our time indoors, out of sight of too many eyes.

So it was arranged that the following day we were to tidy up the hole in the ground, so that there was no sign of anyone having lived there, and in the evening they would come to escort us to our individual lodgings. They were as good as their word, as usual. We walked into the village and I said cheerio to Jim and Sid and I went with Angelo and his mother to their house. It was, I suppose, a typical peasant's abode. I have already described it, from the evening that we went to get our haircut. Amerigo, the father of Angelo, was there and greeted me with a handshake and a cigarette. I recall that he also said that I was not to be '*pauro*' – that is, frightened. I felt that if anybody at all should be frightened it should be them, because in allowing me to be in their home they were risking far more than I was. I might be risking my freedom, but they were really risking their lives just to help me.

In Angelo's house there was no place that I could sleep and I discovered that I was to have my food with Angelo's family and then sleep elsewhere. I slept in a house in the village square, the layout of which was most peculiar. My bedroom was simply an addition to the house and to reach it I had to leave by the front door and go round the side of the house in order to enter the bedroom. To go back into the house, I had to reverse the procedure. The bedroom had a window looking out on to the track that ran around the back of the village. The lady of the house was called Giuseppina, but her surname I cannot recall. She told me that her brother was in the Italian army, that he was on the Russian front and she had had no news of him for a long time. It brought home to me that the worry and suffering that the war had brought to so many homes was almost beyond imagination.

Being in close contact with the Marchetti family, all day and every day, I found a great help to me in picking up more of the Italian language. I knew, of course, that grammatically my knowledge was virtually non-existent, but I did find it possible to understand most of what was being said.

I formed the impression that these people really believed that all the people in England were wealthy and I tried to explain to them that I was far from wealthy – indeed I earned my living as a cabinet maker. It was very difficult to explain to them that England, like most other countries in the world, had its rich and middle class and working class. I did manage to get them to understand that I fell into the last group. I must admit, though, that I did recognise that there was a great gulf between the standard of living between the Italian working class and our own.

I must explain at this stage that I was now calling Angelo's mother 'Silietta'. This I suppose was a nickname derived from her proper name of Ausilia. Everybody in the village called her Silietta, so I thought I had better conform. She was a most remarkable woman; her height could only have been about five foot two, and she was quite a plump lady. It seemed to me that there was an almost permanent smile on her face, so she gave one the impression of a being a very jovial lady. Her husband, Amerigo, was a different person entirely. He appeared to have the worries of the world on his shoulders. He was always very pleasant to me and didn't seem at all worried about my presence in his house – this despite the fact that, should I be discovered there by the Germans, he would no doubt lose everything he possessed. He was at all times a very kind and caring person and there were many occasions when I was to be given an insight into how much he cared for his jovial wife.

Being confined to indoors had, after a few weeks, become almost unbearable to me. I would sit and converse with Silietta (after a style) for hours on end and she taught me literally hundreds of words in Italian. Many of them were of course in the local dialect, but these hours thus spent were going to prove extremely useful in the future. One day, Silietta handed to me a '*bi denti*' – this was a tool similar to a pick except that it had two teeth, as the name implies. She said we were going to do a little '*zappire*' – which is 'digging'. I was all for this as it meant that we would be going outside. Fresh air, after the last three weeks, was going to be very welcome.

She took me up the mountain at the back of the village. We passed a number of villagers on the way who all greeted me with '*Bongiorno, Alfredo!*' which made me wonder why it was felt necessary for me to be kept inside the house all the time, when it seemed that quite a lot of people knew who I was and with whom I was staying. However, we carried on scaling the mountain, until we were several hundred feet above the village and then Silietta called a halt and said: '*Ecco*' – which means 'here'.

Pointing to a particular spot she told me to start digging and I was told to dig '*mezzo metro*', which I knew to be a half a metre. As I got down to the required depth, she instructed me to '*Andare piú lentamente*' – which meant to go more carefully, so I complied with her instructions and started to just scrape at the soil, all the time wondering what I was going to discover. I was soon to find out. It was a round object about eighteen inches in diameter and nine inches deep and it was really black. I lifted it to the surface and Silietta asked me if I knew what it was, and I had to tell her that I had no idea at all. When she replied that this was '*buono formaggio*', which meant that I had just dug up about fifty pounds of cheese. I asked her how long it had been buried and she replied that it had been there for about five months and it would be very mature and tasty. After struggling back down the mountain with this weight, I was glad to reach the village once again. On reaching her home, she trimmed all the black rind off and cut into it. She cut off a small portion and passed it to me and in all honesty I must say it was the tastiest piece of cheese I have eaten in my life. It was just wonderful!

It was shortly after this that Silietta was to receive news of her eldest son, Alarico. He had been captured in North Africa and was now in a prisoner of war camp in the United States. She was absolutely over the moon with this news; she was so relieved to learn that he was safe and well. I think that every living soul in the village came to her house to help her rejoice and of course the wine was flowing copiously.

I can remember thinking at that time, What of my family and my girlfriend? They had heard nothing of me for at least six months; how long would it be before they would have news of me? I realised, of course, that this was something that I should not dwell upon. To keep it in the forefront of my mind would not help as there was absolutely nothing I could do about it. It was a very sobering thought.

Silietta now used to sit and cry when I sat at her table having a meal. When I asked her why she was crying, her answer was that she just hoped that Alarico would be given food by his captors. I used to assure her that the Americans were a very wealthy nation, that they had an overabundance of food and materials of every description and that there was little possibility of their prisoners not being reasonably well fed in the American prison camps. I must add that I said this with my tongue in cheek, because I had no way of knowing how Alarico was being treated. If my own experience of food supplied in Italian prison camps was anything to go by, then perhaps he would be meeting with some difficulties.

Angelo was to become my chief supplier of cigarettes; he did this by chatting up German soldiers whenever the opportunity arose and scrounged them for me. If those soldiers had known who was to ultimately smoke the things they would have had a fit!

It was about this time, towards the end of January, that Angelo's friend, a young fellow called Davida who was the son of Pasquale and Bettina, came to the house one evening and told us that he had come across another British prisoner in the mountain, behind the village. He was holed up in one of the shepherd's huts and was very wary of coming down into the village. Davida's parents had already arranged for a family to take him in and, as the weather was by now extremely wet and cold, would I care to accompany him and Angelo the following morning, to persuade him that it was safe for him to come into the village? I agreed at once, of course.

So, in the morning the three of us set off up the mountain once more. It was really great to be out and about. I found myself thoroughly enjoying the climb. When we reached the hut he was not to be seen, so we assumed that he must have moved on to pastures new, and began to retrace our steps to the village. As we were passing a dry stone wall (one that we had passed on the way up), up popped this chap, wearing a blue trilby hat and a jacket and trousers that had almost as many patches as my own. He greeted us with a '*Bongiorno*' that I was at once to recognise as pure Cockney.

It transpired that his name was Tommy Welch and that he

came from the Hackney Road. A typical Londoner if ever there was one. What had happened to him was a story that deserves retelling. He had been making his way to the front and had walked into a unit of German artillery, who had imagined him to be Italian. They trotted out their chap, who spoke Italian to talk to him and it took about half a second to discover that Tommy was not Italian. He admitted that he was British and that he was an escaped prisoner of war, so they bundled him into a nearby shepherd's hut and posted a sentry outside. After a while they brought him some coffee and food and told him that their '*oberst*' or colonel would be coming to see him. He was left alone for about two hours and then the door was opened and there was the Colonel. He dismissed the guard and said to Tom in perfect English: 'Come, let us walk.'

During the stroll with Tom, he praised his escape attempt and said that the English were only about twelve miles further on but that it would be very foolhardy indeed to even think of crossing the lines at this point because of the very high concentration of German troops all around and forward of his positions. He would of course have to return Tom to his prison, as that was his duty, and he walked Tom back to the hut, shook him by the hand and wished him good luck. Tom said that this officer then strolled off and left him in the hut with the door wide open and no guard to be seen. So he was off like a rabbit, back the way he had come. He'd been walking north for about three weeks.

Who could give an explanation for the action of that German officer? Tom couldn't, although he was more than grateful for it. It does seem inexplicable but, on thinking back to my own capture, I remembered the German officer on that occasion and how he shared out our cigarettes and tins of milk between us and his own men.

It didn't take long for me to persuade Tom to give up trying to exist up in the mountains, because these conditions were by now becoming really too tough to be living rough. He came back down to the village with us and Davida took him off to the family, who were going to take care of him. We now had, to my certain knowledge, seven Britishers in the village, and, while one could only marvel at the courage of the people who were giving us shelter, I was pretty certain in my own mind that it would be wiser to move out of the village at the earliest possible chance. I talked this move over with Jim, and after a little persuasion he agreed with me that there were just too many POWs in the place for it to be at all secure for us. We agreed that as soon as the weather became a little better we would be off. By now it was getting near to the end of February and we both thought that the worst of the winter was behind us. However, events were going to make our minds up for us.

About a week after Jim and I had this chat, I had gone to my bedroom on the village square. I've already explained that this room had no access to the house and that it had a window that overlooked the back track that ran around the village. I had climbed into bed and was soon sound asleep. I was awakened by a lot of shouting in German and I was out of the bed like a shot, clad only in my shirt. I went through the window and it was my good fortune to find that right in front of me was a stack of roof tiles. I got close up to these and made myself as small as possible. Meanwhile, the shouting was still continuing and a couple of shots rang out. After about ten or fifteen minutes, the din died down and I heard footsteps coming down the back track. It was a clear, frosty night and I peeked over the top of the tiles and saw the Germans moving off with two of the prisoners, whom I recognised as Les Law and Norman Hartley. A few minutes later I heard the engines of their trucks start up and drive away. I now realised that I was shivering – in fact, I was almost frozen. Imagine leaping out of a nice warm bed with nothing but a shirt, then jumping out of a window on a cold and frosty night! No wonder I was shivering! So I climbed back through the window, thinking that, as they had raided the village, they were not likely to do it a second time on the same night. So I climbed back into bed to try to restore my circulation. I must admit, though, that on that particular night I had no further sleep.

Early the following morning, I got myself dressed and left my bedroom to amble over to the fountain to splash some water on my face and the villagers who were about went berserk. They were telling me, '*Scappate immediatamente perché i tedeschi sono arrivati ieri sera.*' In English, I was to escape because the Germans had come the evening before. As if I was unaware of that! They were, of course, quite right – I should be off straight away. I couldn't endanger them for another moment. So with their cries of 'Good luck!' ringing in my ears, I headed once more for the mountain behind the village.

After climbing for about an hour, I was to meet up with the first of my fellow fugitives: it was Sid Courtney. He had been roused from his bed and told to scarper by the family caring for him. He had needed no second bidding, merely stopping to put his trousers on. I told him I had seen Les and Norman being escorted off by the Germans. He was unaware of this but of course not really surprised that they had bagged somebody, because the village was really overpopulated with our chaps. I told Sid that it was my intention to move back into the hideout that was in the copse of trees down by the road. He agreed with me that it was a good, well-hidden place and he would join me. So we set off together.

We hadn't been travelling for more than half an hour when we met up once again with Jim. I was delighted to find that he had made it out of the village. His story was much the same as ours, except that his family had filled a bag full of food for him: bread, cheese, nuts and some salami sausage. Wonderful people! So now there were three of us to muck in together to try and stay one step ahead of the Jerries. We settled in our old hideout once again. Within a couple of days, Angelo and Davida had found us. They told us they had been right along the top of the mountain, looked in all the caves and huts and were beginning to think that we had gone farther afield. I told them that, having raided the village, the Germans would probably be thinking that, if there were any more prisoners, they would be scared to be anywhere near that particular village. So we would be fairly secure where we were – we hoped!

Chapter Ten

Angelo had arranged our food supplies once again and the evening visits to us by the ladies were, of course, the most welcome thing in the world for us. I know that I was becoming quite happy to tuck into a bowl of their peas; these were a regular meal that was brought to us and they were very nourishing indeed. Always they left a little something that would see us through to the following evening – some bread, cheese and a little fruit. Whenever Angelo accompanied them, he invariably brought along a few ciggies to share among us. These were nearly always German and were of course the result of Angelo's scrounging on our behalf.

We could still observe the road, and the vast majority of the traffic was German. We noticed that the greater volume of this was still moving after dark. This was readily understood because we were now into March and the weather was much milder and the days were beginning to lengthen. It was noticeable that air activity was on the increase in a very big way. Every day now we were watching quite a number of our fighters zooming about in the skies. Our confidence was beginning to rise and we began to think positively that we just might have a happy outcome to our trials and tribulations. Then something happened that made us feel really down in the dumps.

It was a wedding in the village that caused us to be so miserable. This sounds strange, I know, but what happened was this. The wedding was in the family who were looking after Sid Courtney. They had taken him into the village to be rigged out into some decent gear, because they wanted him to attend the reception in the evening. He returned to the cave looking quite smart and spent the afternoon trying to keep himself clean and tidy for the evening's celebrations.

At around 6 p.m. they came out from the village to take Sid in for the party. It was to be forty years before I saw him again. It transpired that at some time during the evening an Italian at the party realised that Sid was an Englishman and had slipped out and informed the Germans, who turned up and of course took him away. When the people of the village told us about it, this being about thirty minutes after he was recaptured, we were out of that place incredibly fast with Angelo's words ringing in our ears: we were to be very careful because this, he said, was the work of a '*spia*' or spy.

So once more we took to the mountains. Jim and I were really upset about losing Sid like that even though, on reflection, it was a pretty foolhardy thing to do. It brought it home to us that we must not become too complacent; we must still keep our heads down. We were, after all, still escaped POWs and we just had to keep on our toes.

We climbed for about six hours and it must have been about 4 a.m. when we called a halt. We were both pretty well played out, really tired and exhausted. I can recall Jim saying, when we arrived at this particular shepherd's hut, that he didn't give a damn if it was full of fleas and that once he had shut his eyes they wouldn't bother him. I was not prepared to argue with him and within a few minutes we were both sound asleep.

It was mid-afternoon when I woke up and, not disturbing Jim, I got up and put my head out of the door. I saw that we were in a pretty large clearing in the mountain that was well grassed. Up behind us, some half mile or so distant, was a pretty thick forest of trees. It was a glorious spring morning – quite a nip in the air, but sunny and bright. I realised that it was 12 March, my birthday. It was my twenty-fourth birthday. I knew that my folks at home would be thinking of me on this particular day and they had no way of knowing whether I was dead or alive. A very sombre thought! Whilst I was full of these thoughts, Jim came out of the hut and joined me and just at that moment we were treated to a lovely sight – six aircraft were approaching from the mountains at the end of the valley. They were weaving all over the sky, displaying beautiful red, white and blue roundels. Jim and I were cheering our heads off. It was a very heartening sight. We weren't to know it then, but this was about to become a very common sight in the days and weeks to come. I must confess, though, that after losing Sid the day before, it did the world of good to our morale and gave us a renewed feeling of confidence.

We spent four days at this particular hut and we had virtually exhausted our little stock of food, so it became imperative for us to move once again, to find sustenance of some sort from somewhere. We agreed that we would have to get lower down if we were to find food; it would be very unlikely for us to stumble upon a village at this height. We packed our few belongings and set off once again down the mountainside. How nice it was to be walking downhill instead climbing!

Our descent from the mountain was comparatively easy. It was a really fine spring day and we were approaching familiar territory. We were nearing the region of the villages we both knew so well – the huge area of land shaped like a triangle with the villages of Collebrincioni, Pettino and Arischia at its three points. We had already agreed to reoccupy the cave on top of the mountain behind the village of Pettino, providing that it was vacant. We reached this cave, I remember, at about midday and shortly after we were to be greeted by our old friend Maurizio, the shepherd from Arischia. He gave us a little food that he happened to have with him and said we were too great a distance from his village to supply us with food regularly, but he would get word to Angelo of our whereabouts. True to his word, the following afternoon Angelo was spotted making his way up to us with some very much needed supplies. He gave us all the latest news of where fighting was taking place and told us that the Allied forces had mounted a huge air raid on the airfields at Foggia. He said that the airfields were completely destroyed. We were able to verify this later – it was perfectly true. So we had got some accurate information at last!

A couple of weeks passed by with a great deal of air activity by the RAF, who seemed to swoop out of the skies and shoot up almost everything that moved on the roads. We were sitting in a small group of shrubs, which afforded us a good view of the track, when Jim drew my attention to two figures that were heading our way from the direction of Arischia. The closer they got, the more apprehensive we became, because they were in uniform and well armed and we did not recognise the uniform. Before we could move, we realised we had been seen; they waved to us, halted and signalled to us to approach them. This we did and the shorter of the two asked us, in a kind of Italian, who we were and what our business was in the mountains. Meanwhile his companion was covering us with an automatic weapon. I tried to reply in my fractured Italian, when Jim suddenly said to me: 'Are they Germans?'

I can remember the reply of the shorter man to this day: he said that he hoped not! Immediately it was established that we were indeed all English, and Jim and I were really and truly brought up to date with the news. It turned out that these two were members of the SAS. They had been dropped by parachute in the north of Italy, near Genoa, and their mission was to destroy a viaduct carrying mainline trains. The mission was a complete success apart from one aspect, and that was that after completing the job they had to make their way to a certain position at the coast on a certain day. They were to be taken off by submarine. If the submarine did not show, they had to return in three days to the same spot. On neither day did the submarine show up, so they started to walk south towards the front. Their journey down from Genoa to where we were in central Italy, in uniform, fully armed, was an achievement in itself. The officer's name was Captain Wedderburn; the other one, who was a corporal, was only ever referred to by the Captain as 'Tanky'. I never did know his real name.

The officer had a great deal of money on him, which he told us was to buy their way out of trouble. We chatted for some two or three hours and gave them to understand that we thought they would be better served by getting out of uniform and into civilian clothing, because the area between ourselves and the front was teeming with Germans. We suggested that they stay with us for a while, saying that we would try through our Italian friends to obtain them some civilian clobber. This they agreed to do and they stayed with us for a couple of days. We had contacted Angelo about them and he made arrangements for them to be found accommodation in Coppito, which was a much bigger village down in the valley.

We did not see them for about two weeks and our next

meeting was very unusual. Angelo came out to us one day and said that the Captain had invited us over to Coppito to have a meal with him, and we all three would be going over there on the following evening. Angelo assured us that he knew a way in to the village that avoided the road and said that we would not be spotted. Upon arrival at this house in Coppito, we were greeted by the Captain and Tanky looking very smart indeed. They were both wearing new suits, natty shirts and ties, and looked like a couple of prosperous people.

The house was crammed with Italians and we sat down to a really fine meal with plenty of wine flowing. There was much back-slapping and toasts to the Allies and it really was a shock to us after the way we had been living for the last seven or eight months. It seemed so unreal, almost as if the war was already over and won. Our trio left the party at about 11 p.m. and made our way back to our cave. I remember that Jim and I agreed that we would not be undertaking a venture of that sort again, as it really involved taking too great a risk.

We never saw the Captain and his partner again – although after the war I was reading a book, whose subject was the infamous German prison camp at Colditz, and the name of a certain Captain Wedderburn was mentioned. I've often wondered if it was the same man. He certainly was a great character and gave one the impression that he could overcome any difficulty. It was pretty obvious that his companion Tanky thought that the Captain was really great.

Having been in this particular cave for a couple or three weeks, Jim and I decided that a move would be to our benefit. We had no reason to suspect that anybody who knew of our whereabouts would betray us to the Germans, but equally you could never be absolutely sure. We gathered up our few belongings and started hiking in the general direction of Cansatessa, because we intended to take up residence once again in the underground place that was about one hundred yards from the main road. We had told Angelo of our intention to move and he, once again, saw to it that our food supplies were well and truly organised. To Jim and me, this young man was our salvation. We could never be able to repay him for what he had done for us.

Once more we settled in to our rent-free accommodation underground and we noticed that things had changed a great deal. By day on the road hardly anything moved; if it did, it got shot up very rapidly. The Germans now only moved their transport by night and many and often were the nights that the valley was to be lit up by flares and resound to the chatter of the RAF's machine guns and cannon fire. Many vehicles went up in flames and it was pretty apparent that the Germans were having a very lean time. With our hole in the ground being so close to the main road, we were almost on the touchlines, so to speak.

Once more, while all this was going on, we were invited to the home of the Morellis. Again we had a very nice meal and some very stimulating chatter, because Captain Morelli listened regularly to the BBC. What he told us of the battles going on at the east and west coast we could take as authentic. He was a very engaging person and an extremely intelligent one. I noticed that, during the meal with his two sons Lorenzo and Giulio, and the latter's wife Alfonsina, the main topic of conversation was the war, yet, after the meal, he would talk to us on all sorts of subjects and really could keep the flow of conversation going. They were wonderful people.

A few days later we were sitting outside our hideout when we could hear the approach of aircraft. They were swarming about the sky and seemed to be looking for something to move so they could have a go at it. Suddenly they all swooped down, one after the other, and there was the most terrific explosion. We must have been two or three miles from the actual explosion, but we felt the blast, as our clothing pushed on to our bodies. We discovered later that on the other side of Coppito, on the road to Rome, all along the road, under trees, the Germans had an ammo dump and this was the RAF's target. We were told that a number of civilians had been killed in the explosion, many Germans were dead and that the road was in a hell of a mess.

It was shortly after this that a very strange event was to occur. We had a visit from Angelo, who told us that there was a German deserter up on the mountain beyond his village, that he was being looked after by some Italians from the village of Collebrincioni and that he was with two English prisoners. We questioned

Angelo as to how long this German had been up in the mountains and he replied that he didn't know. We decided to leave well alone. It sounded a very fishy story to me and altogether too risky to introduce ourselves to a German, especially at this stage, when things were beginning to move at the front. However, we were to meet, and it was only a few days after Angelo had told us about him.

It came about like this. Jim and I knew where there were some fruit trees, pears and apples, about three miles from the village of Arischia, and we decided to go up there and get in a supply. We arrived at the spot and were busy picking some fruit when we saw two men coming towards us. They had seen us so there was nothing to be done but to face them. One spoke to us in Italian and we knew at once that he was English; the other at first said nothing. This chap was from a camp called Macerata. We had heard of this camp. We told him which camp we were from and then he introduced us to his companion. It was the German deserter.

He had a very interesting story. His name was Arthur Glasser and he came from Mannheim. His home had been bombed and his parents and only sister had been killed. He was a transport driver, taking materials up to the front. He was courting an Italian girl, whose village was extremely poor and had completely run out of flour. He stole a truckload of flour and delivered it to the village. For this act he was court-martialled and his sentence was that he was to be posted to a punishment battalion stationed permanently at the front. On arrival at the front, he had deserted almost at once and had returned to the mountains in the L'Aquila region.

He was an engaging character with a very devil-may-care attitude to things in general and his life in particular. Jim and I decided that we did not wish to be too closely associated with this chap. He could be exactly as he represented himself; on the other hand, he could also be something quite different. So we shook his hand and that of his companion and bade them farewell and good luck. Then we returned by a roundabout way to our hideaway down the road.

During the time that we had been out of the camp, we had

met all sorts of people from many different nationalities. They were all of one mind in trying to avoid the Germans and were mainly concerned with reaching our own people at the front. Jim and I often talked of all the turmoil that was going on all around us and we would often ponder on how many of those people that we had met who were indeed heading for the front had been successful, and how many had been recaptured and were once again behind barbed wire. We both agreed that our first priority was to avoid being captured once again, and to do that we had to avoid meeting up with the Germans. If we did move off to the front, then the chances of coming face to face with the enemy were that much greater. We felt that now we were in the month of May and things were beginning to move on the east and west coasts, we should remain inconspicuous until there were signs that the Germans were on their way back. Once we saw that this was happening, we would make our move south.

The weather now was very good, warm and sunny, and we had got into the habit of leaving the hideout very early in the morning and making our way over the mountain behind the village of Cansatessa. The climb took us about two hours and from the crest we had a magnificent view of the valley, with the city of L'Aquila nestling in the centre. The roads from our viewpoint were like black ribbons; the strangeness of this was that they were almost totally deserted. Only an occasional truck or motorbike could be seen. It would appear that all transporting of supplies to the front was a nocturnal happening. Our aircraft were very busy indeed during the day. We would see fighters swarming about nearly all day, and heavy formations of bombers, flying very high, heading for somewhere up north to deliver their loads.

Just beyond the crest of this mountain was a water trough, fed by a stream. This was used by the locals for their animals. The water was always crystal clear and for Jim and I this became our bathroom. It was very cold, but wonderfully refreshing. We often wondered what we would do if we were to be caught in the act of bathing by the locals, but fortunately for us this never happened. It also served us as our laundry. We would wash out an item of clothing, lay it on the ground to dry in the sun and put it back on before we returned to our little underground bedroom.

June was now with us and it was a real scorcher of a month – the sun was shining from dawn to dusk and the temperatures were very high indeed. Jim and I used to leave our hideout just before dawn, head up to the top of the mountain and settle just beyond the crest, where we had a panoramic view of the whole valley. We would lie up there and talk on just about every subject under the sun. The main topic was always the predicament we found ourselves in. On reflection it does seem strange that we never seemed to talk about being recaptured. I don't know whether subconsciously the subject was taboo, or maybe we were both supremely confident that we would not be caught once again.

From our vantage point, we had a bird's-eye view of everything that went on below us on the roads. The Germans were few and far between during daylight. This was to be expected because the Allied air forces were to be seen all day and every day, droning across the skies, looking for a target, with the bombers flying higher in very heavy formations, on their way, no doubt, to a specific target. It would seem that things were now beginning to move where military matters were concerned. We had received the news that a very big battle was going on at Monte Cassino and it looked as though a push was being made to link up with our forces, who had landed at Anzio. We could see that if this ended in success then our forces' next stop was to be Rome. Heavy fighting was also reported on the River Sangro, so all this sort of news made our spirits that much higher. What we could not know was what a long and bitter battle it was all going to be.

Meanwhile we kept ourselves fit with our daily climbs up and down the mountain. Silietta kept up our food supplies. Bettina came along with her occasionally and brought us a few goodies. She still had the Scotsman she called Carlo hidden in her house. We saw Angelo almost every other day and he invariably had some German cigarettes for us. He used to tell us to be very careful, because he was convinced that it would not be long now before we were all liberated and rid of these *tedeschi* once and for all.

Chapter Eleven

June passed into July and we were still in our same hole in the ground near the road. By night we could see that the traffic on the road was increasing, and it was heading north, much to our delight. Angelo came out to us with the news that Sulmona, which was about twenty miles south of L'Aquila, had been occupied by the British and that the Germans were blowing up the power pylons at Popoli, which was about twelve miles from L'Aquila. We quickly decided to leave our hideout and get to the top of the mountain, where we would be able to see well down in to the valley to see what was going on.

When we arrived at the top we had a wonderful view of the pylons, going down to our right, north of L'Aquila. It seems that they were not destroying them all – just doing enough damage to cause some havoc. After we had been up there for a while, we suddenly realised that it had become extremely quiet, so we started to come down lower. We reached the track that went round the back of the village and were face to face with a military truck, one that we had never seen before. We stopped and stood to the side of the track; the truck came on and stopped beside us. They had our tin hats on. They were British! Jim and I were over the moon. Here we were in our old, patched, peasant clothes, explaining to the officer who we were and what we were doing, i.e. dodging Germans. He congratulated us on our escape, gave us some cigarettes, took our names and addresses and promised to write to our parents, which he did. He then told us that L'Aquila had been taken by our troops that morning.

I discovered when I got home, from the letter he wrote to my parents, that it was a Lieutenant EG Hammond, 69 Airfield Construction Group, 8th Army. I still have the letter.

We wished them good luck and they went on their way. We headed off to the village and found that there was a great celebration in progress. The village square was full of very happy, jubilant people. We started to do the rounds, to thank these people who had been so good and kind to us for so long. When they realised that we were going into L'Aquila to report to AMGOT (Allied Military Government of Occupied Territory) they understood, but were so sorry to see us leave.

We reported in and were received very well and we were put into a hotel, which to us two tramps was like paradise. I know I wallowed in the bath for an hour or so – it was heaven!

We were in the hotel for a week and nothing seemed to be happening, so Jim and I decided to take off and to get further south. We walked down the road towards Popoli and started to try to get a lift on a passing military vehicle. For quite some time, we had no luck at all. Then along came a heavy military vehicle, driven by a cheerful chap, who pulled up to our frantic waving. We explained our position to him and he told us to climb on board and away we went. We journeyed on through Popoli and a few miles further on our driver pulled into a US military depot to fill up with petrol. We were, immediately the centre of attention and were taken to their mess hall and given a very good meal, followed by coffee! An officer then came up to us and took us to a building that turned out to be their equivalent of our NAAFI, and then we were given a carton of 200 cigarettes each, taken back to the truck and we were once again on the way to Naples.

When we reached Naples, our friendly driver wished us luck and dropped us off. So here we were, still in our old patched-up civvy clothes and looking like a couple of tramps, wondering what we should do next. Naples was packed out with military personnel and was teeming with their traffic. We passed a building and a British Navy officer came out, so we approached him and told him all about ourselves. He took us into the building and made a telephone call. When he had hung up, he came over to us and said we were to wait outside the building and a vehicle would pick us up in about ten minutes. He then shook our hands and wished us luck.

As he had said, after ten minutes a truck arrived which turned out to be the Military Police. Once again, we had to explain who we were and how we had managed to arrive in Naples. Then we were asked to get into the truck and we were on our way to who knows where. We arrived at an MP depot and we were taken into an office and told to sit down. After a couple of minutes a captain came in and we had to once again repeat our story to him. He explained to us that he was running a detention centre. I pointed out to him as that we had been behind barbed wire for two and a half years and behind enemy lines for ten months living off the land we had had our share of barbed wire. He was very sympathetic and agreed that the detention centre was not the place for us and he would see what he could arrange.

He called in an orderly and told him to take us to the mess hall. We were to be given a meal and something to drink and then we were to be brought back to his office. We were both beginning to feel much more at ease. About an hour later, in the Captain's office, he told us that he had arranged for us to be taken to a rest camp at Salerno. We both expressed our thanks to him for his efforts on our behalf, to which he replied, 'It's nothing, lads; you have more than deserved it.' He was, indeed, a nice chap.

When we arrived at Salerno, we were interrogated. They wanted to know everything about us: name, number, rank, unit, division, when captured, where captured, date captured, which camps we had been in, when we escaped. The answer to the last one question was September 1943. The officer expressed surprise and asked were we sure of the date, as it was now July 1944.

Jim spoke up: 'Yes sir, we spent ten months evading recapture because we did not wish to go to Germany. We just wanted to be where we are today – with our own people.'

We were taken to the quartermaster's stores, given a denim battledress, underwear, soap and a towel, and then to the ablutions for a bath. Then we were off to see the MO for a medical examination. We were then told to report to the stores the next day to be fully kitted out. We spent three or four weeks at this rest camp in the joyful knowledge that we were only waiting for a passage home. We could also write home for the first time for almost a year. This alone raised our spirits no end. At last came the day when we were told to go to the office and the good news was given to us. We were given an embarkation card and told to be ready to board the trucks to Naples at 9 a.m. the next day.

The reader cannot imagine how elated we were feeling – we were simply walking on air! We duly climbed aboard the truck next morning and soon arrived at the docks in Naples. Our ship was the *Empress of Bermuda* and she was bound for Britain – our joy was complete.

The voyage was uneventful and we finally docked in Liverpool, we were taken to a place called Eastham, just outside. We spent two days there for medicals and documentation and were then sent home on leave. We arrived in London and walked to the Central Line underground station. After our ride on the Tube, Jim and I were to part, because I would be getting off at Leytonstone and Jim was going on to Woodford, but first we arranged to meet up a couple of days later.

I got on a bus with full service marching order and asked the conductress for a penny fare to the Thatched House pub. She replied that Id been away a long time, because the fare was three pence! As I went to get some change out she said: 'Have this ride on me!'

I got off the bus at the Thatched House and, as I knew that my parents had moved house whilst I had been away and I knew that it was near the pub, I looked around for somebody who could tell me where their new house was. I asked a bus inspector who was standing there if he knew where the road was.

'Have you just got home?' he asked. I answered that I had.

He told me that there had been a doodlebug down there. He asked me my name and whether I was Buller's son. I told him I was, then he told me the family were all right and were in accommodation, which was temporary – somewhere, but he did not know where.

I was reunited with them eventually and I discovered that my younger brother Charlie was in the Navy, out in Trincomalee, and my youngest sister was an evacuee up in Wigan. My sister Ann was the only one at home and she was at work. The following morning I decided to go over to see my girlfriend, who lived in Leyton, and her mother greeted me as she was the only one at home. We had a long chat. Then she asked me if I would like something to eat and I replied that I would. She asked me what I would like and I replied that I would like egg and chips.

After those years of macaroni soup and rice soup this simple dish was something I had yearned for. It was delicious! Shortly after I had had my meal, my girlfriend, Violet, came home. Now she worked with her father in Bishopsgate Station and here she was home, about four hours early, so how had she found out that I was home? The grapevine had worked. It was a moment that I will never forget, a moment I had dreamed of for the past three and a half years.

My mother told me that she had had two soldiers visit her a couple of months previously and it turned out to be Bobby Dodge and Clicker Clarke, my old mates. That was good of them, because my family had had no news of me for almost a year. At least they now knew that I was alive.

I didn't meet up with Bob and Clicker until after the war. I believe it was in 1941 that Joe Drew, who was a great character in the camp at Sulmona, organised our first reunion at a pub in Stockwell. It was so good to be back in company with those two lads once more. As can be imagined, we spent much time recalling the situations we had found ourselves in, some pretty scary and others rather hilarious.

After about three or four years of holding the reunion in different places we were fortunate enough to be given the opportunity to hold it at the Union Jack Club at Waterloo. In the earlier years at the Union Jack Club, the attendance would be over two hundred. After four or five years, Bob failed to show up, despite the efforts Clicker and I put into trying to get in touch with him. Over the years the number of people attending grew smaller and smaller. The years were taking their toll until finally, in 2004, we held our final reunion. We had in total fifty-one at the club. We were all grey-haired old men, nearly all of us sporting a walking stick. It was sad to say our farewells to each other. Time marches on.

Postscript

I mentioned earlier an escapee that Jim and I had met in the village; we only knew him as the Duke because he was always so much better turned out than us. I think it must have been twenty-five years later when he managed to track me down and the Duke, Frank Meadows, came to visit me at my home. Amazingly I recognised him immediately. It was great to see him again and reminisce about old times. Frank told me that he was still in touch with the Morelli family who had been so kind to Jim and me, but sadly Alfonsina had lost her husband Giulio after a long illness. I wrote to Alfonsina to offer my condolences and a correspondence ensued. She later visited England and came to see us at our home. Later Alfonsina invited Violet and me to visit her, first at her apartment in Rome and later at her country home in Pettino. A lovely time was had by all, so it was with sadness that I heard from her daughter much later that Alfonsina had passed away. Her kindness and that of her dear husband Giulio will never be forgotten.

Jim Kerr and I had a lifelong friendship. Our families holidayed together and to my girls he was always Uncle Jim.

My dear friend Clicker Clarke and I met up again very soon after the war and remained very good pals, attending for many years our official reunions at the Union Jack Club in London and making a return visit to our old camp in Sulmona, Italy. This trip turned out to be far more than expected. We were welcomed like old friends by the Mayor of Sulmona, were wined and dined and each presented with a commemorative medal (as shown on the front cover). A great trip, very much enjoyed by all of us.

My family's friendship with the Marchetti family continues to this day. We have holidayed with them in Italy, and Angelo and his wife Teodalinda (or Linda) left Italy for the first time to celebrate their twenty-fifth wedding anniversary at our home. It is a long and valued friendship born out of kindness and gratitude.

Due to demand, our Annual Reunion has been revived, so the few of us who remain still meet up once a year. Sadly we lost the original instigator, dear Joe Drew, in June 2007 so I will just reiterate Joe's last comment at the end of each reunion:

Will the last man standing please turn the lights out?

Printed in the United Kingdom
by Lightning Source UK Ltd.
130579UK00001B/24/P